Smart Tips for Estate Planning

For the LOVE of FAMILY

Marvin Toy
Jim Yih

Think Box Consulting

Editorial Director: Neil Sawers
Photography: Kim Carmicheal and Marvin Toy
Cover Design: Jim Yih

Smart Tips for Estate Planning
Copyright © 2008 Marvin Toy and Jim Yih

All rights reserved. Printed in Canada. No part of this work covered by copyrights herein may be reproduced or used in any form or by any means – graphic, electronic or mechanical – without the expressed prior written permission of the publisher.

For information address: Think Box, 7505-104 Street, Edmonton, Alberta, Canada. T6E 4C1
www.thinklots.com

Care has been taken to trace ownership of copyright material contained in this text. The publisher will gladly receive any information that will enable any reference or credit line to be rectified in subsequent editions.

This publication is specifically designed to provide accurate and authoritative information in regard to the subject material covered. It is sold with the understanding that the author, publisher, and Think Box Consulting Inc. are not engaged in rendering legal, accounting, investment planning or other professional advice. The reader should seek the services of a qualified professional for such advice. The author, publisher, and Think Box Consulting Inc. cannot be held responsible for any loss incurred as a result of specific investment planning decisions made by the reader.

FIRST EDITION

Printed in Canada

About the Authors

Marvin Toy, B.Comm, LLB. Marvin is a lawyer who has practiced in the fields of tax law and estate planning over the past 12 years. As a practicing lawyer, he served the clients of Felesky Flynn, LLP, the leading tax law firm in Alberta. He has also provided estate planning, estate settlement, and trust administration services to the clients of CIBC Trust Company and MD Private Trust Company (a trust company exclusively serving medical doctors and their families). He has guest lectured for the Canadian Bar Association and the Faculty of Law at the University of Alberta. In his tax and estate planning work, he has strived to make these difficult subjects easier for his clients and his colleagues.

Jim Yih, B.Comm, PRP, CSA. A familiar face to many, **Jim Yih** is one of Canada's leading authorities on retirement, investing and personal finance. He has become a source for the media as his analysis and research have been sought after by the *Globe and Mail, The National Post, The Edmonton Journal, The Calgary Herald, The Montreal Gazette, The Vancouver Sun, Investopedia.com* and many other publications across Canada.

In addition to being a popular presenter and speaker, Jim writes a regular syndicated column for *The Edmonton Journal* and other *CanWest* papers. His column can also be found at *Canadian Business Online, FundLibrary.com, The Canadian Investment Journal* and the *Canadian Money Saver magazine*.

Jim has authored two other books; the best seller, **Mutual Fundamentals** and **Seven Strategies to Guarantee Your Investments.** Most recently, Jim has created a software program called **My Estate Organizer**, which is a tool designed to help people take the most crucial first step in estate planning – getting organized. This book is intended to work in conjunction with *My Estate Organizer.* For more on Jim, visit his personal website www.JimYih.com.

Smart Tips for Estate Planning

Acknowledgements

This book is dedicated to our parents:

Grant and Susan Toy
Jenn Ching and Lorraine Yih
Bob and Barb Willman

Further acknowledgements are provided to those who have shared one of the most profound secrets of successful professional life – that knowledge is best shared widely and generously.

Disclaimer

This book provides estate planning ideas and concepts. It is intended as an introduction to the subject only, and not as a comprehensive guide. In estate planning, you are dealing with your entire life's savings and the financial future of your loved ones. You will not learn everything you need to know about estate planning just from reading this book. Laws and rules that affect estate planning vary all across Canada and change as governments come and go. You are strongly advised to obtain professional advice before acting on anything you read in this book.

Contents

A. Essentials of Estate Planning
1. Introduction — pg 9
2. Getting organized — pg 18
3. Get your legal estate planning documents done! — pg 22
4. Understand the power of trusts — pg 25
5. Avoiding the probate process and probate taxes — pg 30
6. Writing your Will: do-it-yourself or hire a lawyer? — pg 32
7. How to find good professional advice — pg 35
8. When is the right time to do your estate planning? — pg 39
9. Estate planning for the separated or divorced — pg 43
10. Dying without a Will — pg 46

B. Giving to the People You Love
11. Leaving assets to your spouse — pg 51
12. Creating a spousal trust in your Will — pg 57
13. Leaving assets to your children and grandchildren — pg 62
14. Creating trusts for your children in your Will — pg 65
15. Leaving assets to your parents — pg 79
16. What happens to my pet? — pg 81
17. Can I leave something for my friends? — pg 82
18. How do I leave money for charity? — pg 83

C. Key People in Your Estate Plan
19. Choosing an executor — pg 87
20. Choosing a trustee — pg 93
21. Choosing a guardian — pg 95

More Contents

D. Dealing with Specific Assets

22. Who should I name as beneficiary on my RRSP? — pg 98
23. Joint ownership of bank and investment accounts — pg 104
24. Tax free savings account (TFSA) — pg 108
25. Joint ownership of my home — pg 110
26. Dealing with your personal residence in your Will — pg 114
27. What should I do with the cottage? — pg 117
28. Other real estate holdings — pg 123
29. *In trust* accounts for children and grandchildren — pg 127
30. What happens to the RESP? — pg 132
31. What do I do with my corporation? — pg 136
32. Other business interests or partnerships — pg 141
33. Life insurance — pg 143
34. Your heirlooms and precious things — pg 150
35. Loans or advances from you to others — pg 154
36. What do I do with the farm? — pg 157
37. What do I do with foreign assets? — pg 159

E. More Estate Planning Issues

38. Giving it all away while you can — pg 162
39. *Alter ego* trusts and *joint partner* trusts — pg 165
40. Organ donation — pg 170
41. Making your own funeral arrangements — pg 171
42. Dealing with loss of your mental capacity — pg 173
43. Health care decisions — pg 176
44. What is your legacy? — pg 180
45. Concluding remarks — pg 183

A. Essentials of Estate Planning

In this section we introduce the key elements of estate planning, what you should know, some of the pitfalls, and how important it is to commit to estate planning in the first place.

Introduction

Welcome to Smart Tips for Estate Planning.

When you think about estate planning, what comes to mind? For most people, estate planning is about what happens when you die. Where does your money go? How can you minimize taxes? How can you keep more by paying less?

There's an old saying, "There are only two certainties in life: death and taxes". For many people, this probably captures the essence of estate planning and why estate planning is important.

There's no question that estate planning has a lot to do with finance, money and taxes. And it's no wonder that planning is often motivated by these very important factors.

Being professionals in the estate planning industry with over 30 years of combined experience, we find that estate planning is all about families. The minute you have family to worry about is the minute you start to think about estate planning.

Purpose of the book

The purpose of this book is to introduce Canadians to the many ideas and techniques that they can use to protect their families and maximize the wealth they leave behind.

It is also about preserving family harmony and helping families avoid fights and conflict (which happens all too often).

After reading this book, we hope you recognize the importance of estate planning and that we have given you enough knowledge to take the first steps towards planning your estate. We hope to inspire you to action to find more security and peace of mind with your financial affairs.

Knowledge is Power

As the old saying says, "knowledge is power". This book is about giving you the knowledge to make the most with what you have. We hope you find lots of answers to questions you may have about estate planning. Having worked in the estate planning industry for a combined period of over 30 years, we've been asked a lot of questions and this book attempts to cover some of the most common issues Canadian families face with estate planning.

Unfortunately, reading this book will not make you an expert on estate planning. Being an expert requires years of education, lots of practical experience and typically means you are a professional. With investing, for example, there are more opportunities to do it yourself. With estate planning, it is a lot more difficult. Estate planning is one of those areas that typically requires help and advice from professionals whether it be from an estate planner, lawyer, accountant or financial advisor. Think about it - it is pretty tough to draft your own power of attorney, create a testamentary trust or buy the right kind of life insurance without some help from a professional. Since it is more likely that professionals will be involved in your estate planning process, this book is about creating a foundation of knowledge so that you can work with your advisors more effectively.

Successful people rarely hesitate to get professional advice when necessary. Unfortunately, professional help can sometimes be expensive. Although this book will not replace professionals, we believe this book will give you practical ideas to help you save money for yourself and your loved ones.

Misconceptions about Estate Planning

Statistics suggest that 6 out of 10 Canadians do not have a retirement plan. What's scarier is that even fewer have estate plans.

The first misconception about estate planning is that estate planning is only important when you are older. Typically, the older you get, the more you start to think about estate planning because age puts you closer to the reality of death. However, estate planning is important much earlier, such as when you get married, and especially when you have children. The minute you have people that depend on you is when you need to start thinking about what happens if you die. How will the people you love (your family) carry on for the rest of their lives?

The second misconception is that you have to be wealthy to do some estate planning. Whether you have $100,000 or $100,000,000, your money needs to go somewhere. Whether you make $30,000 per year or $300,000, you have to pay some tax. Any amount of money can become a source of problems and can cause conflicts within perfectly normal families. Sometimes it's not even about the money, but rather about possessions, assets and heirlooms

Good planning can help families stay united rather than squabbling over opposing opinions and uncertainties.

Estate planning is about peace of mind knowing that your heirs get the most out of your estate in a manner that is timely and efficient. Estate planning is about getting organized so you have the control, freedom and independence to make good sound decisions when you are mentally capable of doing so.

In our view, estate planning is essential.

What can Estate Planning do for me?

Estate planning is not just for people who are old or have lots of money. Estate planning is for everyone. Here are some of the things estate planning can do for you:

1. Taking care of you
Estate planning is not just deciding what happens when you die. It is also about taking care of you if you become incapacitated by senility or illness whether through old age or a disabling accident. This is why you need an Enduring Power of Attorney and a Health Care Directive to make sure someone is in place to take care of your financial affairs and your health care if you can't do it yourself.

2. Taking care of your family
After your death, this means making sure the people you love get as much of your estate as possible and in the most helpful way possible. As most people have learned, simply handing over money does not equate with love nor does it equate with taking care of someone. Good estate planning is about keeping families together especially during the difficult emotional period of grieving.

Unfortunately, it does not take much to ignite family feuds. We have seen so many situations where big fights are caused by little things like incomplete intentions, out-of-date instructions, feelings of inequality, and meaningful possessions that can't be divided. It is amazing how a little planning, thought and action can help avoid family conflicts.

3. Protecting your estate from creditors
Before your family gets anything from your estate, the people you owe money to must be paid first. Sometimes you know your creditors, but other times you don't. For example, if you die in a car crash that injures or kills other people, then those people or their estates may become your creditors. There are steps you can take to make sure that your family gets some of your assets before your creditors. For example, designating beneficiaries on

registered plans and life insurance, holding investments with insurance companies, and owning assets with joint ownership can help creditor-proof these assets.

If one of your heirs is deeply in debt, then an inheritance from you could be seized to pay their debts. You can use a trust to make sure that your beneficiaries' creditors don't get the inheritance you leave.

4. Minimizing income taxes at your death

As mentioned, there are only two certainties in this world – death and taxes. In Canada, the federal and provincial governments have gone one better: they have made death an opportunity to collect income taxes. There are two types of income taxes that become payable upon your death:

- Capital gains tax - Upon death, the government pretends that you have sold everything. Consequently, you will have to pay income tax on any capital gains. Capital gains taxes can be avoided when you leave your assets to your spouse or a spousal trust. You don't have to pay capital gains taxes on your principal residence when you die.

- Tax on your RRSP or RRIF - The entire amount remaining in your registered plans will become income and subject to income tax when you die (unless you leave it to your spouse, or a disabled financially-dependent child or grandchild).

As you can see, death is potentially a very expensive event.

Just to clarify a common misconception, Canada does not have "estate taxes". Estate taxes exist in the United States, but not Canada.

5. Minimizing probate fees and taxes

As if income taxes at death weren't enough, many provincial governments also levy probate taxes or probate fees at death. Basically, your provincial government may take a small percentage (currently less than 2%) of all the assets in your estate at the time of your death. Every province sets its own probate fees. For example, Quebec has no probate tax. Alberta has the next lowest probate fees in Canada – a maximum rate of $400 regardless of the value of your estate. Ontario, British Columbia and Nova Scotia have the highest rates – approaching 1.5% of your estate.

You can minimize probate taxes by moving assets outside of your estate before you die. For example, this can be done before you die by giving assets away or by transferring assets to trusts.

6. Minimizing income taxes for your heirs

By using trusts in your estate planning, income taxes can also be minimized for your beneficiaries. If your beneficiaries are likely to invest their inheritance (rather than spend it), then your death actually offers a one-time opportunity to help your beneficiaries save on their future income taxes.

7. Minimizing estate settlement problems

At the best of times, an estate takes 18 months to 2 years to settle properly. Just by making one or two basic mistakes, your estate could take many years, a lot of heartache, a pile of frustration, and too much money to settle. A well-drafted Will and proper estate planning can help your executor avoid these mistakes.

Why does an estate take 18 months to 2 years to settle? The main culprit is the demands of the federal income tax system. If an executor does everything right, then the executor will file a terminal tax return, an estate tax return a year or so later, and then obtain a clearance certificate. That means waiting for the federal government to process three tax filings before the executor can be sure that all taxes have been paid.

8. Meeting legal obligations to your dependants

All provinces have some laws that allow a dependent of a person to claim something from that person's estate. Failure to meet your legal obligations to your dependants will leave your estate vulnerable to challenges in the courts. In some jurisdictions, there is very little that anyone can do to "challenge your Will" like you see on television. In other jurisdictions, there are laws that do allow people to demand more from an estate than they were given. Your lawyer will advise you to ensure that your Will meets your legal obligations and minimizes the chance of claims being made against your estate.

9. Avoiding government and judicial intervention
You will learn in this book that it is very important to have a Will. Otherwise, the government gets involved and that is one thing you want to avoid. If you die without a Will, provincial legislation will determine what happens with your estate. If you have children under the age of majority, then the government will take control of their share of your estate. The courts will decide who your executor will be, and the courts will decide who will be the guardians of your minor children.

If you die with a Will that does not fully address your estate, then the government and courts will intervene as well.

To avoid government and judicial intervention, it is important to complete your estate planning and revise it regularly as your life evolves.

Light bulb moments

As you read this book, we try to give you as many "light bulb moments" as possible.

A light bulb moment is when the light goes on inside your head and something really makes sense. Something makes you say "Ah ha – I get it!" A moment where you say, "That's me!"

A light bulb moment might also be a moment where you read something you already know but this time it's a catalyst to change.

Why does the light come on sometimes and not others? Timing is everything. Sometimes there are times in your life when different pieces of information are more important. Sometimes you are affected by something called "moments of perspective". For example, when a parent dies, or when a baby is born with an illness, or when you just miss getting into a fatal accident. These are all moments of perspective when you can look at your own life with a different perspective than the one you usually have.

When reading this book, we hope you get many light bulb moments, but if you only get one, then it has made our efforts and time worthwhile. You see, knowledge is power, but only if you do something with the knowledge. You can have lots of knowledge about Wills, but until you actually get a Will drafted, the knowledge means nothing. We simply hope the information in this book is helpful, easy to read and inspires you to make changes in your life, especially when it comes to estate planning.

Terminology

Having a clear understanding of certain phrases will make this book easier to understand. To reduce the confusion of using different terminology in each province (due to provincial laws using different words to describe similar things, and local jargon), this book will use some terms in very specific ways.

Joint In this book, if something is owned jointly, then if one owner dies the other owner (or owners) automatically becomes the full owner of the asset. For example, if a husband and wife are joint owners of their house, then when the husband dies the wife becomes the full owner of the house. This is in contrast to *co-ownership* where if one owner dies, the deceased's share remains a part of the deceased's estate and can be given to anyone else. For example, if a sister and brother are co-owners of a farm and the brother dies, then the brother can decide in his Will that his children should inherit his part of the farm.

Enduring Power of Attorney This is a document that appoints someone to manage your assets and take care of your financial affairs if you are alive but incapacitated. Often this is called a *power of attorney*, but there are many types of powers of attorney and not all of them are effective after you become incapacitated. None of these other types of powers of attorney will be discussed in this book. The specific term for an "Enduring Power of Attorney" varies between provinces.

Health Care Directive. This is a document that appoints someone to make health care and personal care decisions for you if you are alive but unable to do so yourself. This is sometimes also called a *living Will* or a *personal directive*. The specific term for a *Health Care Directive* varies between provinces.

Probate Probate is a legal process that occurs after death. The probate process is intended to prove that a Will is indeed the Last Will and Testament of a deceased person. At the conclusion of a probate process, a court of law grants an executor the power to settle an estate.

Estate settlement After someone dies, there is a lot of work to be done and all of this work is collectively called estate settlement. Doing the work is called settling an estate. The probate process is one part of an estate settlement.

Registered plans Means Registered Retirement Savings Plans (RRSPs) and Registered Retirement Income Funds (RRIFs).

Chapter Two

Getting Organized

To begin estate planning you must first get organized. In fact, if you think about it, being organized is an essential life skill, not just with estate planning.

In the financial world, getting organized is the root of financial success. If you want to get ahead financially, you have to organize your finances. You need a systematic approach to managing cash flow. You need to understand how much money you spend. You need to be aware of your assets and investments. You need to organize your financial statements. Getting organized is the starting point to financial independence and freedom.

Successful estate planning is no different. You need to get organized before you put together an effective plan to accomplish all of your estate needs and goals.

Getting organized for estate planning

When somebody dies, typically a lot of questions come up. Where do you find a copy of the Will? Who is the financial advisor? How many financial advisors are there? How many bank accounts are there? What were the wishes for a funeral service? Who needs to be contacted? Where are the investment statements?

Unfortunately, the one person with all the answers has died. Having an organized estate will not only help you feel more in control of your personal finances but it will also help the people you love who must make decisions at an emotionally difficult time.

Getting organized is all about gathering information so you can provide answers to all the questions while you are still around to provide them. When it comes to estate planning, many people don't know what information to gather and the questions that will be asked when they die. Here is a guideline of some of the information you need to put together to get organized for estate planning

- On the first list, you need the names, and your relationship to, all the people or organizations that you would want to give something to after your death.

- On the second list, you need a list of every asset you have including current values, original costs and the details of any co-owners or joint owners. This would include bank and investment accounts, land, stocks and bonds, life insurance, loans receivable, business assets, and heirlooms and other valuable items

- Another list will be key contacts which may include your lawyer, accountant, and financial advisor(s)

- Another list that is helpful is a list of people you think would need to be contacted when you die. Don't take anything for granted. This might include family relationships, key friends, organizations, etc.

- Another list might be a list of specific assets that you want to give to specific people. Often a Will provides general direction for major assets but if you have meaningful heirlooms that you want to give to specific people, then a list of such personal items is very helpful.

- You should make notes of family relationships, the locations of valuable documents, emergency contact information, and safety deposit box location and key location.

My Estate Organizer

Many financial institutions provide their most valuable clients with special forms to help their clients get organized. We have developed a new software program called **My Estate Organizer.**

My Estate Organizer is a tool that sets the stage for financial, retirement and estate planning. It will help people working with professionals to create great plans and move towards financial independence and peace of mind.

This software helps people organize, diarize and communicate their estate affairs. It is a tool that reduces family conflict, bridges communication between generations, and helps executors and beneficiaries during the difficult time of losing someone they love.

My Estate Organizer is easy to fill-out and -- best of all -- it can be updated as your personal circumstances change.

To learn more about how *My Estate Organizer* can help you start the process of estate planning, visit our website at www.MyEstateOrganizer.com.

Diarize your affairs - The Estate Binder

Once you have all the information you need, you must put it together in a useful format. There are many different ways to do this. One of the most consistently successful strategies is having an estate binder.

The estate binder is exactly that – a binder. In this binder, you should have all of the necessary information, documents and lists to help your family if anything should happen to you. My Estate Organizer provides an easy solution to the Estate Binder by simply printing a final document that can form the foundation of the estate binder. Your beneficiaries, executor or family should know where your estate binder is kept so they can find most of the answers that they will need.

Chapter Three
Get your legal estate planning documents done!

Once you are organized and have all your information put together, you are well on the road towards completing three essential legal documents. From a legal perspective, a proper estate plan is accomplished by drafting three essential documents: a Will, an Enduring Power of Attorney, and a Health Care Directive. All other estate planning decisions, such as beneficiary designations and how you own certain assets, must work in concert with these three legal documents.

Will

The most important of your estate planning documents is your Will. A Will says what happens with all your worldly goods after your death. A Will may include trusts for your loved ones. A Will is used to appoint guardians for your minor children.

In its most basic form, a Will is a document that defines four important groups of people in your estate plan.

1. Beneficiaries. Not only does the Will say who will get your assets after your death, but also specifically which assets each beneficiary will get and how and when your beneficiaries should get those assets.

2. Executor. The Will must appoint someone who has the responsibility to settle your estate. Choosing the right executor is not as easy a task as you might think. This person has a lot of responsibility and should be someone who can handle a difficult task. Your executor should be someone who has some financial experience. Ultimately, your executor should be someone you trust.

3. Trustee. If you are planning to have any trusts set up in your Will, then you will need to appoint a trustee to manage the trusts.

4. Guardians. If you have minor children, it is crucial that you appoint guardians for those children. This, too, is a big responsibility. Obviously, you should ask permission before you appoint someone as a guardian in your Will.

A Will must be written and signed according to very specific rules that are different in every province. While this may seem insignificant, there are many stories about people who did not follow these rules and thereby caused problems in the estate settlement process.

Enduring Power of Attorney

The second formal document in an estate plan is the Enduring Power of Attorney. The Enduring Power of Attorney appoints someone to manage your financial affairs if you are alive but not capable of making financial decisions for yourself. It also sets out that person's powers. The person you appoint is called your *attorney*.

Health Care Directive

The third document essential to an estate plan is the Health Care Directive which appoints someone to make health care decisions for you if you are alive but cannot do so yourself. It may also set out your wishes. The person you appoint is called your *agent*.

Other Things To Do

Although these documents are crucially important, there are other strategies for estate planning outside these formal documents. Other strategies include owning things jointly with other people or naming direct beneficiaries on certain assets like RRSPs, RRIFs and life insurance policies. It may also mean giving away assets during your lifetime or creating trusts before you die.

As part of the estate planning process, start with these three documents and the rest of your plan will follow accordingly.

Chapter Four
Understand the power of trusts

Many people don't know much about trusts because they can be intimidating, technical and complicated. Don't worry because there is really nothing to fear. Trusts, as a legal concept, have been around for hundreds of years, and are well understood by experienced Will, estate, and trust lawyers. Many textbooks have been written about all aspects of trusts, but here is the briefest of introductions to the concept.

A trust is simply a relationship. One person (called the trustee) holds something (the trust property or the trust fund) for the benefit of another person (called the beneficiary). When there is more than one trustee, they are the trustees. When there is more than one beneficiary, they are the beneficiaries.

Ownership of the trust property is divided into two people. The trustee has legal ownership, while the beneficiary has beneficial ownership. Consequently, the trustee has special legal obligations (called fiduciary duties) to manage the trust property solely for the benefit of the beneficiary.

To create a trust, someone such as you (called the settlor) must clearly:
- Intend to create the trust, as shown by creating the trust in a Will or by signing a *deed of trust*
- Identify the trust property by description or a formula, and
- Identify the people or purpose (such as a charity) who will benefit from the trust property.

Property you put into a trust is called *capital*. Investment returns on the capital are called *income*. If income is not distributed to beneficiaries at the end of the year, then the income is added to the capital.

Two kinds of trusts used in estate planning

There are two kinds of trusts that you can create for estate planning purposes:
a) A trust that exists only after your death is called a *testamentary trust*, and
b) A trust that exists during your lifetime is called an *inter vivos trust*.

Why would you create a *testamentary trust*?
- To protect property – by giving legal title to the trustee, the trust property is protected from the creditors of the beneficiary
- To take care of your loved ones – the trustee is legally obligated to manage the trust property in the way you decide
- To obtain income tax benefits for your beneficiaries – if a trust is created in a Will, then income from the trust property is taxed as though it is income of a separate individual (see example below). This is a basic form of *income splitting*.

As you can see, testamentary trusts are all about taking care of other people and should be a serious consideration in your estate planning. In your Will, you can create as many testamentary trusts as you need – for example, one for each of your children, or you can create one trust for all of your children.

Why would you create an *inter vivos* trust?
- To avoid estate settlement and probate processes upon your death
- To limit income tax on capital gains during your lifetime and upon your death
- To minimize probate tax upon your death
- To distribute income from the trust among many people (a complex form of *income splitting*)

But be careful because an *inter vivos* trust also has some negative aspects:
- You lose the income tax benefits of testamentary trusts, and
- Income in an *inter vivos* trust is taxed at the highest income tax rate

Due to these negative aspects, *inter vivos* trusts are much less common in estate planning for most people. However, in the right situation -- such as when you own business assets that are rising in value -- they are still very useful.

Terms of a trust

When it comes to the *terms* (rules) of the trust, you generally have very wide latitude to decide what they are. In a situation where the beneficiary is someone who cannot handle money wisely (for example, due to addictions or disability), then the rules you create might be very strict. On the other hand, if the beneficiary is healthy and wise, then the terms might be liberal and allow for great generosity by the trustee. Discussion of appropriate terms will occur where trusts are recommended.

How a trust can reduce income taxes

Tax rules are always ridiculously complicated. Tax rules for trusts are no exception. Fortunately, there are many tax lawyers and tax accountants who are available to make sure you get the maximum benefits with the fewest hassles.

Briefly, here is an example of how a trust can save your beneficiary income tax after your death.

Jack is the Beneficiary of his mother's estate. He earns $70,000 annual income from employment. His mother leaves him $500,000 of cash that earns $30,000 annual interest income

If you give the money directly to your beneficiary, after one year your beneficiary's tax position . . .		If you put the money in trust for your beneficiary, after one year your beneficiary's tax position and the trust's tax position . . .	
Beneficiary's tax return		**Beneficiary's tax return**	
Employment income	$70,000	Employment income	$70,000
Interest income	+ $30,000	25% Tax on the $70,000	-17,500
Total taxable income	$100,000		
		Trust's tax return	
		Interest income	$30,000
		26% Tax on the $30,000	- 7,800
25% Tax on the $70,000	-$17,500		
40% Tax on the $30,000	-$12,000	Total tax owing	- 25,300
Total tax owing	- $29,500		
		Savings from using a trust	$4,200

This is a very simple illustration using a rough sampling of various provincial tax rates and personal tax credits. A trust is not eligible for personal tax credits, but is eligible for its own set of graduated tax rates. The graduated tax rates produce the savings for the trust.

Expenses of operating a trust

Having a trust does cost some time and money to operate. Here are some of the expenses that may be incurred with a trust.

1. Trustee's fees
   - Regular decisions need to be made about how to invest and maintain the trust property. The trustee is entitled to be paid for the time and effort spent administering the trust. If the trustee is a family member, then the trustee's costs may be nothing. Your trust terms could say how much your trustee is entitled to be paid.
   - If a trust company is the trustee, then the trust company will usually be paid an annual fee based on a percentage of the trust property. The fees for a trust company are usually on a sliding scale (the more valuable the trust property, the smaller the percentage fee) and may start around 2% on the first $1 million in trust property.

2. Accounting fees for tax filing
   - A trust must file a tax return every year. Accounting fees can vary widely depending on the number of beneficiaries. If a trust has only one beneficiary, then the accounting fees should not be more than the accounting fees for a person with similar income.

3. Legal expenses
   - Your trustee should consult with a lawyer every few years to ensure that the trust is running smoothly and the effect of any new laws is considered.

If the main goal of the trust is to minimize tax, simplify estate administration and minimize probate tax, then it is important to consider the expenses of a trust before proceeding. If protection of your wealth and the care of your dependents are more important, then the expenses of a trust are merely a cost of achieving your goals.

Chapter Five
Avoiding the probate process and probate taxes

Nobody likes to pay more taxes than they must. Nobody likes spending money on lawyers and the courts, either. Avoiding the probate process and probate taxes is one reason to do your estate planning. Just don't make it the driving reason.

Doing estate planning solely to avoid the probate process and probate taxes is like choosing the place you retire based solely on the weather. Great weather, like avoiding probate taxes, is wonderful. But in choosing your retirement home, you also want a safe place, clean water, good food, and access to medical care. That's why nobody retires in Burma. If avoiding probate taxes means more income taxes, more problems settling your estate, and more bad blood among your children, then the cost of avoiding probate taxes is not worth the trouble!

The probate process is a legal process that occurs after death and is intended to prove that a Will is indeed the Last Will and

Testament of a deceased person. At the conclusion of a probate process, a court of law grants an executor the power to settle an estate. The probate process involves various expenses; for example, court fees and lawyer's fees. Without a grant of probate, the institutions that hold or register your assets are unlikely to deal with your executor. Those institutions include banks and the land titles office.

You cannot avoid the probate process by not having a Will. If there is no Will, then the probate process is replaced by a legal process to appoint an executor to settle your estate and decide how to distribute it. This process is likely to be more expensive than the probate process.

Probate taxes, if levied by the province where you live, are based on the assets you own at the time of your death.

The only way to ensure that your estate will completely avoid the probate process and probate taxes is to have nothing in your estate when you die. Other strategies to avoid the probate process and minimize probate taxes include:
1. Giving away your assets before you die (directly to others, or by putting your assets into trusts)
2. Naming beneficiaries (other than your estate) on your registered investments, life insurance policies and other investments held through life insurance companies, and
3. Holding your assets jointly with others.

Each of these methods can be appropriate at various times, but each also has potential drawbacks, therefore these methods must be used carefully. Remember, that avoiding probate is only one goal of your estate planning. Don't place too much emphasis on this issue alone.

Chapter Six

Writing your Will: do-it-yourself or hire a lawyer?

Some people say you should never write your own Will. They are usually right. There is really only one situation where it is OK to write your Will without professional help: you have, and always will have, virtually no assets.

Hand writing your Will, whether free-form or using a preprinted "Will kit", sets the stage for a potentially expensive and problematic estate settlement. Banks, government agencies and the courts are rightfully wary of hand-written Wills. The cost of interpreting a hand-written Will by a lawyer and a court is more expensive than paying for a properly drafted Will in the first place.

If you want anyone to benefit from your estate, then hiring a lawyer to write your Will is money well spent. A well-written Will that is customized to your circumstances is a document that can often suit your needs for many years, or even decades.

The key is to hire a qualified and experienced lawyer to help you, one who specializes in Wills, trusts and estates.

Be careful in hiring a lawyer who does not specialize in these fields. Some lawyers will happily draft your Will for you – right after handling your divorce, helping you buy your house, setting up your corporation, reviewing your taxes, and helping you with your car accident. These lawyers are generalists, not specialists.

In many professional fields, there are generalists and specialists. Remember, the Will is the foundation for your estate plan. When it comes to drafting a Will, we believe it is so important to hire a specialist rather than a generalist. Few people can do everything well and lawyers are no different. After all, you wouldn't go to a knee surgeon to get your heart fixed!

Due to the fact that most people have very little experience with trusts, no one should ever attempt to create a trust in a Will or in a deed of trust without the help of an experienced Will, estate and trust lawyer.

Cautionary Tale
Penny-wise, pound foolish

An elderly woman, Sherry decided to write her own Will. She was well-educated and had her full faculties at the time. Although never married or having children, she had a large number of adoring family – including siblings, and nephews and nieces. Mary and Helen were the sisters closest to her.

Through frugality and wise financial planning, she had a significant estate: around $1,200,000. Because of her frugal ways, she did not want to pay a lawyer to write her Will.

When she died, her family found her hand-written Will that said, in part, "1/3 of my estate to Mary and Helen, and divide the rest among my nephews and nieces". Almost all of the relatives believed she meant to give 1/3 of the inheritance to Mary ($400,000) and 1/3 of the inheritance to Helen ($400,000) and 1/3 of the inheritance divided among the nephews and nieces ($400,000).

However, one of the nephews – influenced by his wife and other relatives – thought that the phrase should be interpreted so that Mary and Helen shared 1/3 of the estate. With this interpretation, Mary would receive 1/6 of the estate ($200,000), Helen would receive 1/6 of the estate ($200,000), and the nephews and nieces would get 2/3 of the estate ($800,000). The nephew could double his inheritance with this interpretation.

Of course, no one knows for sure what Sherry meant, but the nephew demanded that the court decide whether his interpretation was correct. Unfortunately, putting the estate through such a court proceeding cost the estate (not the nephew) many thousands of dollars. If Sherry had hired a lawyer to write her Will clearly, the cost would likely have been much lower than the legal costs that resulted from the ambiguity in her Will as well as avoiding uncertainty and family conflict.

Chapter Seven

How to find good professional advice

When you think about it, estate planning is all about people. Not only is it about passing money to the people you love but it's also about finding people to help you though the estate planning process. Unfortunately, finding good help is sometimes easier said than done.

Good estate planning often comes from a team of professionals, which might include:

1. **An estate planner or financial advisor.** The term financial advisor has become a bit of a catch-all phrase. At one time, insurance agents sold insurance, stock brokers sold stocks, banks sold GICs, and financial advisors sold mutual funds. Now everyone is into each other's business. Today, an estate planner is sometimes just a financial advisor that specialized in the field of estate planning. Chances are this advisor has an expertise with life insurance and living benefit insurance with specific application to estate planning. Typically, an estate planner does not prepare Wills or other formal documents of estate planning. As a result, a

good estate planner will work closely with an accountant and a lawyer to create a team of estate professionals.

2. **A lawyer** who can draft Wills but is also versed in trusts and estate settlement. The truth is you can't do a proper estate plan without having a lawyer because they are the only ones that can draft the three essential documents properly.

3. **An accountant** who can help plan to minimize tax and deal with preparing returns after your death. Filing taxes needs to be done each and every year. When someone dies, a terminal tax return and an estate return must be filed; and a clearance certificate should be obtained. Although this can be done by the avid do-it-yourselfer, having an accountant who is used to doing terminal returns and estate returns is invaluable.

Finding the Right Team of Professionals

Assembling the right team for estate planning is no easy task. The good news is that usually when you find one good professional that specializes in estate planning, they probably work with professionals from other fields.

Whether you are looking for a lawyer, accountant or a financial advisor, here are a few tips to help you determine if they are the right person for the job.

- o Specialist vs Generalist – Estate planning is a specialized field and you want to work with specialists.

- o Trust vs. Competence – A good advisor will have both qualities. On one hand, good advisors will have technical competence. In other words, they know their stuff. This typically comes from experience, education and professional training. On the other hand, you must also trust them. This is much more difficult to quantify, but trustworthiness is essential to finding the right professional.

- o The price is right (Value vs. Cost vs. Benefit). Obviously professionals deserve to get paid. Often fees and costs can become a hurdle preventing people from getting things done. As the old saying goes, you often get what you pay for. Thus, it is important to look at value as opposed to just cost. Never be afraid to ask up front how and how much the professional gets paid. True professionals recognize their value and have no problem disclosing fees. Once you have established cost, don't be afraid to ask the professional to clearly describe what services are being provided.

- o Getting referrals. Referrals can come in a few ways. First, ask your friends and others in your community – but only ask those people who have circumstances similar to your own (economically, family-wise, business-wise, or professionally). Second, seek a referral from an existing professional advisor. For example, you might ask your own lawyer. Your lawyer may specialize in another field, like corporate agreements, and be unwilling to write your Will for you. Who would he or she recommend? Who drafted their personal Will? Last, you can find lists of well-respected estate planning professionals chosen by their peer groups. For example, magazines aimed at lawyers and some newspapers occasionally publish lists of the top lawyers in the Will, estate and trust fields.

It is sometimes hard to find a good estate planning professional, but like finding a good mechanic or a good handy-man, taking the time to get good help usually pays off in a job well-done.

Cautionary Tale
The lawyer at church

Aaron and Shona have 2 young children. A lawyer who attended their church drafted their Wills. Both of the Wills said that if one spouse died, then that spouse's assets were divided between the children. Nothing was left for the surviving spouse! The couple said they had noticed the words, but thought that it must have been implied that the surviving spouse would get all the assets. They were wrong. When a good estate planning professional found the error, Aaron and Shona were sent to an experienced Will, estate and trust lawyer immediately for new Wills.

Cautionary Tale
The lawyer with new ideas

Jack was a lawyer who prided himself on having the newest technology, quickest service, and a new format for writing Wills. Although Jack had a high-tech system in place, it was no substitute for experience. From time to time, less common situations came up that did not fit his system. For example, he was not sure what happens with a professional corporation after a shareholder dies. He was also unsure whether land could be put into a trust. Even though Jack was a lawyer who marketed himself as a specialist, he lacked some basic knowledge. After receiving instructions from an estate planner, Jack re-drafted the same Will four times in the next 8 months before it was ready for signing by the client. Drafting Wills is not the place for new packaging and one-size-fits-all products: good estate planning is customizing a solution based on solid principles that have lasted the test of time.

Chapter Eight

When is the right time to do your estate planning?

When is the best time to do some estate planning?

For a Health Care Directive, the moment you are an adult.

For an Enduring Power of Attorney, once you have assets that require decisions – perhaps once you have $100,000 of net worth.

For a Will, once you have assets, a child, or are separated or divorced.

For other things, the moment you purchase any real estate, open an RRSP, or start a business with another person.

The best time to plan is as soon as you can. For example, if you want to retire and make retirement the best years of your life, do some planning before you actually retire, before it's too late. In estate planning, too late is typically when you die or when you are incapable of making important decisions.

Principles of planning

Planning is done in all facets in life. We plan our weddings, we plan vacations, and we plan for retirement. Estate planning is another facet of life that requires planning. Throughout this book, we will help you complete your estate planning. Here are some key principles of estate planning:

Principle 1: Planning is personal. Avoid rules of thumb. Avoid doing things just because others are doing it. The key to planning is doing what is right for you. All planning should be individual so it accommodates your unique circumstances, situations and problems.

Principle 2: All plans should be written. Plans need to be real and concrete. The more real the plan, the more likely it is to come true. Writing a plan makes it real and more accountable. It also helps you to stay focused. A plan is not a plan until it is written.

Principle 3: The sooner the better. Don't procrastinate. Start planning right away. Don't let excuses get in the way. Just get started. Remember it's never too late to start. Remember the Nike slogan: Just do it!

How often should I revise my estate planning?

If your estate planning documents are well written, then they should be flexible and contemplate future changes in your life. Nevertheless, it is a good idea to review your estate planning documents whenever one of the following occurs:

- You get married
- You get separated or divorced
- You live in a conjugal relationship for over a year
- You have a child
- You have a grandchild
- You have a significant new asset

- You anticipate financial difficulties in the future
- You move to another province or country
- Your health deteriorates
- Your child gets married
- Your child gets separated or divorced
- Your spouse or your child's health deteriorates
- Your spouse or your child faces financial difficulties
- Your spouse or your child develops an addiction (alcohol, drugs, gambling)
- Your spouse or child dies
- Your adult child become financially dependent upon you
- Your child no longer has any contact with you
- Your executor or trustee moves to another province or country
- Your executor or trustee becomes elderly, ill, or dies
- Your executor or trustee no longer has any contact with you.

People often ask if there is a set time period within which they should review their estate planning. Should you review your estate planning every year? Every 3 years? Every 5 years? From experience, every year is probably too much: most people don't have significant changes in their life from year to year. The same is true for every 3 years.

However, most people will have something significant happen in their life every 5 years. But if something significant happens in your life, then waiting 3, 4 or 5 years until you update your estate planning could be too long to wait. That's why it is better to keep this list in mind and whenever something significant happens, revise your estate planning.

Changes to your estate planning should be done with the same seriousness and professional assistance as your initial planning. Never hand-write changes on your Will or hand-write a *codicil* (amendment to your Will)!

Cautionary Tale
The adoring Grandmother

Jane is a very happy and active grandmother. She took care of her estate planning a few years ago – after her husband passed away. Nothing had changed in her life since then.

Her two children and five grandchildren were healthy and doing well. She kept herself busy taking care of her youngest grandchild – a beautiful and sunny four-year old girl named after grandma. Jane adored her family and thus estate planning was very important to her.

After reviewing her Will, we discovered her plan to leave a $25,000 gift to each of her four grandchildren and then dividing the remainder among her children. The problem was that she had FIVE grandchildren, not four!

When she signed her Will, the youngest grandchild had not been born. She had named each of the other grandchildren in her Will thinking that no more grandchildren were coming.

Aghast that her lovely little granddaughter was left out of her Will, she immediately made an appointment with her lawyer to revise it.

Two lessons come out of this story. First, make sure your Will is flexible to accommodate changes in your personal circumstances. Second, make sure you review your Will from time to time.

Chapter Nine
Estate planning for the separated or divorced

If you are separated or divorced, the time for estate planning is RIGHT NOW! Do not delay!

One of the last things people think about while coping with marriage breakdown is estate planning. This is a huge oversight.

Being separated does not change marital rights if one person dies. If there is no Will, then the spouse could be entitled to all or a portion of the deceased's estate. If there is a Will, it is still in effect even after divorce. So if you have an old Will that gives everything to your spouse, then you may want to change that immediately!

You also want to change your Enduring Power of Attorney and Health Care Directive immediately – especially if your separated spouse or ex-spouse is named as the person who has the power to manage your assets and make your health care decisions!

Cautionary Tale
The terrible car accident

A woman was separated from her husband and they had school-aged children. She suffered a severe and permanent debilitating brain injury in a car accident.

Her husband filed for divorce. In the divorce proceedings, he demanded full custody of the children, plus child support. After extensive court proceedings, where her relatives – none of whom lived in the same city – tried to protect her interests, the husband was successful. The court ordered that monthly payments be made from her assets to him.

Could proper estate planning have prevented the rather ridiculous situation of a brain-injured mother paying child support to a healthy and employed ex-husband? We will never know, but surely proper estate planning would have reduced some of the incredible strain on her relatives.

Cautionary Tale
Steve gets only a fraction

Steve is an adult whose mother and father separated over ten years ago. Steve's father later remarried, then Steve's father passed away this year. Before his death, Steve's father had promised he would leave his *investments* to Steve, and that his stepmother would *take care of* Steve and his sister.

Steve's father never wrote a Will, and when he died almost all of his assets transferred over to his new wife because the assets were owned jointly with her (including the bank accounts and the house) and she was the beneficiary of his RRIF. The only remaining asset was an investment account with $280,000.

Since Steve's father died without a Will, provincial legislation required that the investment account be divided between the new spouse and all of Steve's father's children – which included Steve and his sister <u>and</u> the two children from the second marriage.

In accordance with the provincial legislation, Steve received one-fourteenth of the amount in the investment account ($20,000). Steve's stepmother had no legal obligation to provide anything else to Steve (or his sister), and chose not to give them anything else.

In the absence of a Will and proper estate planning, Steve's father failed to provide for Steve as he had promised.

Chapter Ten
Dying without a Will

Many people die without ever having written a Will. When that happens, provincial laws and the courts decide who will settle the estate and who will benefit from the estate. The provincial laws usually divide the estate between the deceased's closest family. In theory, this can sound like a good thing. In practice it may produce quite undesirable outcomes.

When you die without a Will, you are said to die "intestate". That means provincial legislation governs your estate. This legislation has a very limited scope of action, and its standard provisions may be unacceptable for your personal needs and peace of mind. This may cause potential problems and is very risky for the loved ones you leave behind. Plus, there is no executor appointed, which leads to costs, delays, and frustration.

9 consequences of dying without a Will

If you don't believe just how important it is to have a Will, then think about these 9 consequences of dying without one:

1. Without a Will, you do not have an executor. Therefore, someone must be appointed to act as an administrator of your estate. This means potential delay, expense, frustration, and even losses to your estate.

2. There is no opportunity to select guardians for any minor children you may have. This means that the Public Guardian (the government) may be involved in your children's personal lives. Any parent knows how important it is to make sure that your children are in the hands of someone you know and trust.

3. Your children may not receive the inheritance you want them to receive, and there is no opportunity to provide a trust for them. If your children are minors when you die, this also means that when they reach the age of majority they will receive their entire inheritance in one lump-sum rather than spread out over a reasonable period of time.

4. The Public Trustee is involved in the administration of your children's share if they are minors. This means the government will decide your child's financial future. The government will also take a portion of their inheritance as the government's fee.

5. In the event of a disaster where your entire immediate family dies, your estate may go to a relative that you may have never spoken to, or don't even like. Instead, with a Will, you may make provisions to create a legacy through charitable giving in the case of a common disaster, or choose another suitable beneficiary.

6. Without a Will, there could be more problems for people who were in common-law and same-sex relationships. Provincial laws have not kept up with the ever-expanding variety of relationships. It is especially important for people in non-traditional relationships to have a Will to protect their loved ones.

7. You are unable to take advantage of tax savings and save money on lawyers and court costs following your death. The cost of drafting a Will is so much lower than paying legal fees when there is no Will.

8. Do you want your estate to go to your grandchildren if their parent (your child) predeceases you? Only a Will can ensure your wishes are carried out in the event a family member dies.

9. Without a Will, a family business or family heirloom may not be kept in your family. When you own something of significant value - like a business or other unique asset - it is very important to plan ahead to avoid potential conflicts, and avoid a forced liquidation of your assets.

Ultimately, without a Will, you are unable to exclude or include various people as your beneficiaries. Without a Will, your family and loved ones are left to the mercy of the law, the government and the courts.

Cautionary Tale
Parent with young children dies without a Will

Rick and Susan have two young children. Rick dies without a Will. Does Susan get all her husband's assets? Believe it or not, the answer is no.

Rick's estate will be divided relatively equally between Susan and the two children. (Susan will get a preferential share of $40,000 to $200,000 depending on the province where they live.)

Since the children are minors, their part of the estate becomes the legal property of the provincial government (the public trustee). The public trustee now has the legal obligation to manage the money until the child reaches the age of majority. Until then, Susan must apply for money from the public trustee to care for her children. Does any mother want to ask the government for her husband's money to pay for her children's living expenses?

When each child reaches the age of majority, no one can stop the child – who would be 18- to 19-years of age depending on the province – from receiving full control of his or her inheritance. Imagine if the inheritance is significant – even as little as $200,000 – would anyone really want an 18-year old to have $200,000 in cash?

Parents must have Wills!

Cautionary Tale
Single person with divorced parents dies without a Will

Judith is a very successful woman in her thirties. She is single and has no children. She has a close relationship with her mother, sister and brother. She has no contact with her father who abandoned the family decades ago.

If Judith dies, provincial laws will require her estate to be divided equally between her mother and her father! Her siblings will get nothing. To ensure that her father receives no part of her estate, she must have a Will.

Often, people think if they are single and have no dependents, they do not need a Will. For Judith, that is clearly not the case. Even single people need a Will.

Smart Tips for Estate Planning

B. Giving to the People You Love

In this section, you will find tips, strategies and information on how to give your estate to the people you love. Remember estate planning is all about giving so here are some thoughts about giving to different people that are important in your life.

Chapter Eleven
Leaving assets to your spouse

No book can tell you what you should leave to your spouse. The right answer will depend on your relationship, and the financial needs of your spouse and your children, among many other factors. Every situation is unique and personal. That being said, regardless of your particular situation, some considerations are universal.

A spouse is someone to whom you are married. For the purposes of this book, it also includes a *common law* partner, which means someone you have lived with in a conjugal relationship for a year, as well as same-sex couples. For same-sex couples, the rules are still evolving so we recommend professional advice.

When you are leaving assets to your spouse, there are two key considerations to take into account:

1. Understand that there are significant deferrals of income tax available by leaving assets to a spouse. These deferrals are not

usually available if you leave those same assets to any other person. Leaving assets to a spouse has significant benefits in the estate planning process.

2. You want your spouse to receive assets as easily and as quickly as possible after your death. Many estate planning strategies are not just about minimizing tax but also about maximizing the efficiency of transferring assets to your spouse. Some assets are best passed to your spouse through the Will while other assets are best transferred outside of the Will through beneficiary designations or joint ownership.

Here are some thoughts and suggestions on which circumstances are more appropriate for different assets.

Leaving assets outside of your Will

RRSP/RRIF
Consider making your spouse the beneficiary of your registered plans. RRSPs allow you to designate a beneficiary when you set up your RRSP at a financial institution. This can save income taxes on your death, keep this asset away from your creditors, and keep it from being part of your estate for probate tax purposes.

Life insurance
For similar reasons, you might want to make a life insurance designation that names your spouse as the beneficiary of your life insurance policy.

Bank accounts, investments accounts, and your home
Consider making all your bank and investment accounts into joint accounts with your spouse. Similarly, think about making your spouse a joint owner of land, especially your home. Consult a tax accountant or tax lawyer before doing this with existing accounts or land titles to make sure you don't inadvertently incur an income tax liability.

Tax Free Savings Accounts (TFSAs)

If the option is available to designate a beneficiary when you set up your TFSA at a financial institution, then you should consider making your spouse the beneficiary. This may have the benefit of keeping this asset away from your creditors, and keeping it from being part of your estate for probate tax purposes.

Using the Will to leave assets

In your Will, leave everything else to your spouse if that is your intention.

If it is your intention to leave some of your estate to your spouse and some of your estate to other people, then, as much as possible, structure your Will so that you leave assets with unrealized capital gains (such as shares in corporations and land) to your spouse and assets without unrealized capital gains (such as cash and life insurance proceeds) to the other people. This will minimize the capital gains taxes payable on your death.

<u>Sample Estate Plan</u>
Close to retirement

A husband and wife, married for 35 years, have three adult children who are all healthy and employed.

They own their home jointly. They own their bank and investment accounts jointly. Each has named the other as the beneficiary on their RRSPs. They also own vehicles, household goods and personal items.

Each Will for the husband and wife says:
- The first choice for executor is the spouse, and the alternate is the oldest of their children
- Upon the death of one spouse, all that spouse's assets are distributed to the surviving spouse
- Upon the death of the last surviving spouse, all the assets are divided equally between the three children.

This is an example of a very simple plan in a very simple situation.

Sample Estate Plan
Second marriage with children from first marriage

In his second marriage, Dan is married to Nicole. Dan has two adult children from his first marriage and none from his second marriage. His children live independently from him.

His assets consist of:
$400,000 townhouse (which he fully owns)
$80,000 RRSP (his children are beneficiaries)
$100,000 life insurance policy (Nicole is beneficiary)
$10,000 savings account
$60,000 mutual funds

In his Will, Dan leaves the mutual funds to his children and everything else to his wife.

Dan's plan could be set up to be more tax efficient. If he died with the present situation, his estate would have to pay tax on the RRSPs (assume 40% tax on the $80,000 or $32,000 in tax) and on any capital gains on the mutual funds (for example, $4,000). After his death, the distribution of his estate would look like this:

Nicole:
- $400,000 townhouse
- $100,000 life insurance proceeds
- <u>$10,000</u> savings account
- $510,000 total

Children
- $48,000 from RRSP
- <u>$56,000</u> mutual funds
- $104,000 total

Total estate after tax: $614,000

With tax-efficient planning, Dan would switch things around to make Nicole the beneficiary of the RRSP and the children the beneficiaries of the life insurance. He would also switch things around to leave the mutual funds to his wife and the savings account to his children. By doing this, there would be no tax payable on the RRSP and the mutual funds on his death. After his death, the distribution of his estate would look like this:

Nicole:
- $400,000 townhouse
- $80,000 RRSP
- <u>$60,000</u> mutual funds
- $540,000 total

Children
- $100,000 life insurance proceeds
- <u>$10,000</u> savings account
- $110,000 total

Total estate after tax: $650,000

With this new plan, both Dan's wife and his children receive more assets and the government receives no income taxes.

Although that may be good planning to minimize taxes on the estate, it is also important to be aware of future income tax issues for Nicole. Although Nicole gets more assets, she is also inheriting the deferred tax liability on the RRSP and the mutual funds. In other words tax-efficient estate planning is great – but not perfect. When Nicole dies, her estate will get taxed on the RRSP and mutual funds (unless she remarries). Ideally, however, if Nicole is in a low tax bracket when she spends the RRSP and mutual funds during her lifetime, then the cost of the deferred tax liability will be less than if she died with the assets.

Chapter Twelve
Creating a spousal trust in your Will

When you die and leave some money to your spouse, you don't have to give the money directly to your spouse. You can leave it to your spouse in a *spousal trust*. An experienced Will, estate and trust lawyer can create a spousal trust in your Will.

A spousal trust is a special type of trust that must conform to rules in the Canadian *Income Tax Act*. If these rules are met, then a transfer of assets into the spousal trust upon your death will occur without capital gains taxes. The rules require your spouse to be entitled to receive all the income from the trust, and that no other person can benefit from it.

There are a number of circumstances when you should consider using a spousal trust:

- If you want your spouse to save taxes on the income earned on the money you leave
- To protect the money from your spouse's creditors
- If you have children from a previous relationship
- When your spouse does not manage money well
- When your spouse has, or may have, debt problems

You can leave any assets you own to a spousal trust. However, assets you own jointly with someone else (even your spouse) will not go into the trust because they will pass to the joint owner upon your death.

Registered plans can go into a trust, but they will be taxed on your death if you do it, so this is rarely done (except when your spouse is incapable of managing money or had debt problems).

Aside from the terms required by the rules in the Canadian *Income Tax Act*, you can decide the other terms of the spousal trust. For example, you can decide when income is distributed or not, and when and how much capital is distributed. Distribution of income and capital can be restrictive or generous depending on the situation of your spouse. The idea of a spousal trust is well known to experienced Will, estate and trust lawyers so don't hesitate to raise the possibility with your lawyer.

Here are some example terms of a spousal trust:
- The spouse is entitled to receive all of the income from the trust (mandatory term)
- No person, other than the spouse, may receive any benefit from the trust before the spouse's death (mandatory term)
- The trustee has the unfettered discretion to distribute the capital of the trust to the spouse, or
- The trustee may distribute the capital of the trust only for the medical needs of the spouse, or
- The trustee shall generously distribute the capital of the trust for the benefit and advancement of the spouse.

Another consideration in a spousal trust is to determine who will receive the remaining trust property after the death of your spouse. Being able to make this decision is particularly useful if you want the remainder to go to children from a first marriage, for example. The downside can be that your children may wait a long time to get this remainder. Often, a parent of children from a prior relationship will make other provisions in the Will for those children.

Choose a trustee

Choosing a trustee is an important part of creating a spousal trust. Some lawyers believe it is OK for the spouse to be the only trustee, but this could allow tax authorities to deny that a trust exists. Can a trust really exist if the trustee and beneficiary are the same person – especially if the trustee can fully distribute the trust property to the beneficiary? To reduce the risk of tax problems, having another person as trustee, or as co-trustee with the spouse, is recommended.

A trust for your spouse that is not a *spousal trust*

It is possible to create a trust for your spouse that does not meet the requirements of a spousal trust. No avoidance of capital gains taxes will occur for the assets transferred into this trust. If the assets going into the trust had no unrealized capital gains (such as cash or life insurance proceeds), then the avoidance of capital gains taxes is irrelevant. However, other benefits of a trust, such as protection from creditors and income tax savings on trust income, are still available.

There could be good reasons for creating a trust that does not meet the special rules of the spousal trust – for example, if you need a trust for your spouse and your children.

Sample Estate Plan
Spousal Trust - Close to retirement

Harold and Ally have been married for 35 years. They have three adult children (two sons and a daughter) who are all healthy and employed. Harold's wealth is significantly higher than Ally's.

They own their home jointly. They own their bank accounts jointly. They also own vehicles, household goods and personal items.

Ally has an investment account with $150,000 in bonds and GICs. Harold has an investment account with $1 million in stocks.

Each has named the other as the beneficiary on their RRSPs (including the wife's spousal RRSP).

Ally's Will says:
- The first choice for executor is her husband, and the alternate is the oldest son
- Upon her death:
    o her investment account is divided among her three children
    o her jewelry is given to her daughter, and
    o all of her remaining assets are distributed to her husband.
- If her husband has predeceased her, then all her remaining assets are divided equally between the three children.

Harold's Will says:
- The first choice for executor is his wife, and the alternate is the oldest son
- The trustee is the oldest son
- Upon his death:
    o his investment account is transferred to a spousal trust, and
    o all of his remaining assets are distributed to his wife.
- The terms of the spousal trust are:
    o the trustees are his wife and the oldest son

- - his wife is entitled to receive all of the income from the trust
  - only his wife may receive any benefit from the trust during her lifetime
  - the trustee shall distribute the capital of the trust generously to his wife, and
  - upon his wife's death, all remaining assets are divided among his children.
- If his wife predeceased him, then all his remaining assets are divided equally between his three children.

With this spousal trust, the husband has provided the opportunity for lower income taxes by splitting the future income tax bill between his wife and the spousal trust.

Chapter Thirteen
Leaving assets to your children and grandchildren

Just as no book can tell you what you should leave to your spouse, the same can be said for what you should leave to your children. The right answer will depend on your relationship with your children and grandchildren, the financial needs of your spouse and your children, and the laws in your province, among many other factors. That being said, regardless of your particular situation, some considerations are universal.

Leaving assets to children outside of the Will

Unlike with your spouse, the use of joint accounts and joint ownership of land is rarely advisable. Aside from potential income tax issues and risking your assets to your children's creditors, many children have fought over the true ownership of assets that were held jointly between a deceased parent and one child to the exclusion of other children.

Listing your children as beneficiaries on your registered plans like RRSPs or RRIFs is also not recommended, especially if your children are minors.

Naming children as life insurance beneficiaries may be OK, but only if the children are responsible adults. For minors or children with personal issues, a life insurance trust may be appropriate.

Leaving assets using the Will

One of the most common things done in Wills in Canada is to say that upon the death of the last parent, all the remaining estate is divided equally among the children of the deceased. There is nothing wrong with this at all. However, it is an old solution to the problem of dividing an estate that misses many opportunities to help your children.

Today, in Canada, trusts in a Will are such a powerful tool that anyone writing a Will should seriously consider creating trusts to leave assets to their children.

When should you consider leaving a child's inheritance in a trust?

- If your child is a minor
- If your child is young and inexperienced with money
- If your adult child does not manage money responsibly
- If your child has a gambling problem
- If your child wants to save taxes on the income earned on the money you give
- To protect the money from your child's current or future creditors
- If your child is, or could be, in a marriage that could end in divorce
- If your child is, or could be, in a "common law" relationship that may not be permanent
- If your child has a drug or alcohol addiction
- If your child has a physical or mental disability.

A trust can provide benefits to a child in any of the above situations compared to simply giving your child an inheritance directly. Given the comprehensiveness of the above list, it is obvious that you should always consider using a testamentary trust for a child.

How much money do I need before I should consider a trust for a child?

If your only goal is to provide future tax benefits to your child, then you probably need more than $250,000 to make the income tax savings greater than the costs of operating the testamentary trust (assuming no trustee fees).

However, if you have any other goals, like protecting the inheritance, then any amount of money is worthy of being held by a trustee. Would any amount of money be well-spent if given directly to a child with a gambling problem or drug addiction? Probably not.

Chapter Fourteen

Creating trusts for your children in your Will

(Also applicable to grandchildren and nephews and nieces)

When you die and leave some money to a child, you don't have to give the money directly to your child. You can leave the money to your child in a trust.

A trust for a child is useful in many situations. One common misconception about trusts is that trust funds are only for people from rich families. Anytime you leave money for a child, you should consider using a trust.

In particular, a trust is especially useful whenever a child cannot handle money responsibly.

Trusts for children and young adults

Parents should create trusts in their Wills if they have minor children or their older children are financially inexperienced. A trust will protect a child's inheritance and financially support the child.

Many people think a trust for a child will give the child the entire trust fund at age 18. What do you think an 18-year old would do if given a $250,000 cheque? A $1,000,000 cheque? What if this 18 year old recently lost one or both parents? What temptations would appear – fast cars, luxury clothes, expensive nightclubs? How many self-interested people would be pleased to help your child spend an inheritance in these ways? Would spending money be more fun than studying diligently at university or working hard for a living? The main idea of a trust is that a trust helps you to protect your child's inheritance from potentially bad choices.

Whenever young or financially inexperienced children are part of a family, the parents should put each child's share of an inheritance in a trust. We recommend making the trust last until the child is at an age when the child is more financially responsible. In many cases, we think that age is between 25 and 35 years old (but definitely not always the case).

It is also important to give the trustee the power to hand out money to pay for the child's education, medical needs and living expenses, or whatever you were already providing for your child.

The trustee takes your place when it comes to handing out money to your child. Do you want your child to have money to travel once out of high school? If so, add this as a term of the trust. Do you want to pay for your child's wedding or coming-of-age ceremony? If so, add this as a term of your trust.

Sample terms of a trust for minor child or young adult

- The trustee shall have the discretion to distribute income and encroach upon capital for the education, health, benefit and advancement of the child

- Further encroachments as follows:
    - 1/3 of the capital in the trust at age 25 years
    - ½ of the capital in the trust at age 30 years, and
    - The remaining capital in the trust at age 35 years.

With these terms, the trustee can spend trust property to take care of your child until age 35, if necessary.

It also gives your child three chances to have roughly equal lump-sum amounts of the inheritance. If the first two lump sums are spent unwisely, then hopefully any lessons learned from wasting money will be learned before the last distribution is made at 35 years of age.

- If you believe that holding the money in trust until age 35 is too restrictive, then change the capital encroachments to:
    - Half of the capital in the trust at age 21, and
    - The remaining capital in the trust at age 25.

- If you believe that holding the money in trust until age 35 is not restrictive enough, then change the capital encroachments to:
    - 1/3 of the capital in the trust at age 40 years
    - ½ of the capital in the trust at age 50 years, and
    - The remaining capital in the trust at age 60 years.

- The trustee may provide the beneficiary with up to $10,000 for the purpose of international travel after the beneficiary's 18th birthday.

- The trustee may, in its absolute discretion, pay any expenses relating to the beneficiary's wedding to a maximum of $20,000.

As you can see, you can customize the terms of a trust to suit your desires. All you need to do is tell your lawyer what you want, and your lawyer will draft the appropriate words to add to the terms of the trust in your Will.

Sample Estate Plan
Young couple with young children

Roger and Cindy have been married for five years. They have two healthy children and may have another child.

They own their home jointly. They also own their bank accounts jointly. They also own vehicles, household goods and personal items.

Roger has no beneficiary named on his RRSP. Cindy has her mother named as beneficiary on her RRSP. They are planning on going to their financial institutions to change the beneficiary designations to each other.

Each Will for Roger and Cindy says:
- The first choice for executor is the spouse, and the alternate is Cindy's father
- The trustee is Cindy's father, and the alternate is Cindy's brother
- The first choice for guardian is Cindy's brother, and the alternate is Cindy's sister

- Upon the death of one spouse, all that spouse's assets are distributed to the surviving spouse
- Upon the death of the last surviving spouse, all the assets are divided equally between separate trusts for each of their children
- The terms of the each trust are:
  - the trustee may distribute income and encroach upon capital for the education, health, benefit and advancement of the child until the child reaches age 35 years old
  - further capital encroachments as follows: 1/3 of the remaining capital at age 25 years, ½ of the remaining capital at age 30 years, and the remaining capital at age 35 years
  - if a child dies before age 35 years, then any children of the child become the beneficiaries; if there are no children of the child, then it is distributed to the child's siblings.
- If no parent or child survives, then all remaining assets are divided into two parts: one part is given to Cindy's parents, and the other part is given to Roger's parents.

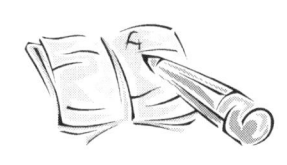

Sample Estate Plan
Single parent with young children

Karen is divorced and has two healthy minor children from the marriage. She and her ex-husband share custody of the children.

Karen owns her home. She has a bank account. She also owns vehicles, household goods and personal items. She also has an RRSP with her children named as beneficiaries. She is planning to go to her financial institution to change the beneficiary to her estate.

Karen has an insurance policy with her ex-husband named as beneficiary. She is planning to go to her insurance company to change the beneficiary to her estate (or an insurance trust).

Karen's Will says:
- The first choice for executor is her best friend Kathy, and the alternate is her brother Marc
- The trustee is her best friend Kathy
- Her choice for guardian, if the children's father is dead, is her cousin, Gina
- Upon her death, all the assets are divided equally between separate trusts for each of her children
- The terms of the each trust are:
    - the trustee may distribute income and encroach upon capital for the education, health, benefit and advancement of the child until the child reaches age 35 years old
    - further capital encroachments as follows: 1/3 of the remaining capital at age 25 years, ½ of the remaining capital at age 30 years, and the remaining capital at age 35 years, and
    - if a child dies before age 35 years, then any children of the child become the beneficiaries; if there are no children of the child, then it is distributed to the child's sibling.
- If no child or grandchild survives, then all remaining assets are distributed to her parents and their heirs.

By doing this, she can ensure that her ex-husband never receives any part of her estate.

If you are thinking about creating a trust for a grandchild or a nephew or niece, then you should be gently urging the child's parents to do their estate planning, too. Valuable information like this should be shared!

Trusts for a disabled child

A physically or mentally disabled child may never be able to manage money. For this child, create a trust that:
- Never distributes lump sums
- Protects the inheritance and financially supports the child for life.

To create a trust in your Will for a disabled child, you need to make sure you hire a lawyer who knows how provincial disability support programs work and how trust funds interact with these programs. The size and income of a trust for a disabled child can reduce the amount of support payments the child receives.

Example terms of a trust for a physically or mentally disabled child:
- The trustee shall have absolute discretion to distribute income and encroach upon capital for the education, health, benefit and advancement of the child
- The trustee shall have absolute discretion to distribute income and encroach upon capital to provide for the comfort of the beneficiary
- The capital of the trust shall be managed to last for the lifetime of the beneficiary
- The trustee may purchase an annuity for the beneficiary.

In some jurisdictions, you cannot avoid the fact that any amount in a trust for a child will reduce the child's eligibility for government support. In these situations, some parents will leave nothing, or only the minimum legally required amount, to the child. The remainder of the estate is left to another person (the child's sibling, for example) with the informal understanding that the person will use the money to benefit the child. This is not always advisable. The care of the disabled child may be compromised if the healthy sibling who is informally providing for a disabled sibling dies or gets divorced or has money trouble.

Trust for a child with alcohol, drug or gambling addictions

Like a disabled child, an addicted child may never be able to manage money. For this child, create a trust that never distributes lump sums so that the inheritance is protected and is available to financially support the child for life.

The trust can pay the child's housing costs (rent, utilities) directly, so the child can never squander this money. The trust can provide small amounts of cash regularly for other living expenses.

Example terms of a trust for a child with addictions would be the same as for a disabled child.

Trust for a child with money problems

If your child is deeply in debt or is always spending more money than is earned, then create a trust than never distributes lump sums. Create a trust that protects the inheritance by giving money only at the discretion of the trustee. Or, create a trust that distributes a monthly stipend.

Example terms of a trust for a child with addictions would be the same as for a disabled child. Further examples:

- The trustee may pay a monthly sum to the beneficiary not to exceed $2,000, or a similar amount adjusted from time to time for increases in the cost-of-living.

If the child's financial difficulties may be temporary, then . . .
- The trustee may distribute income and capital to the beneficiary in the trustee's absolute discretion.

Trust for a married child

Many marriages do not last. If you worry that your child's marriage won't last, and you don't want your future ex-son-in-law or ex-daughter-in-law to get the money you leave for your child, then create a testamentary trust in your Will. In particular, create a testamentary trust that protects the inheritance by giving money only at the discretion of the trustee.

Some advisors say that a trust is overkill because matrimonial property laws in some provinces state that the inheritance of one spouse is not divisible in case of a divorce. However, this is true only if the inheritance is not inter-mingled with marital assets. Once the inheritance is used in the marriage – for example, placed in a joint bank account, or used to pay a mortgage – then the inheritance is no longer exempt from division in the divorce. Practically, without a trust, it is difficult for someone to completely keep an inheritance away from his or her spouse. To prevent these problems, do your child a favor and put the inheritance in trust.

Example terms of a trust for a married child:
- The trustee may distribute income and capital to the beneficiary in the trustee's absolute discretion
- The trustee shall distribute income and capital generously to the beneficiary in the trustee's absolute discretion.

Trust for a grandchild

For many reasons, a parent may decide that a child should not inherit anything, but that a grandchild is deserving of an inheritance. Sometimes, a grandparent wants to provide an inheritance directly to a grandchild.

Whether you decide to skip a child, or provide an inheritance to both a child and a grandchild, you can do it. You can put the grandchild's inheritance in a trust with terms appropriate to the grandchild's circumstances.

Trust for a financially responsible adult child

A testamentary trust has income tax saving benefits for a child who is financially responsible. If your financially responsible child has provided you with grandchildren, then the benefits of a trust are multiplied.

You can create a trust for your child and the grandchildren, and give the trustee the discretion to give out the money to any of them. This trust can be used to save lots of income tax on the earnings made on the inheritance. This is an income-splitting technique. Income tax savings can be obtained by having income taxed:
- In the trust (rather than in the hands of your child), and/or
- In the hands of your adult grandchildren when they have little income (such as when they are attending post-secondary education).

If this type of trust is properly drafted and the trustee is well chosen, then your child (and your grandchildren) will be able to receive money from the trust whenever needed, or leave money in the trust to achieve the maximum tax advantage.

Since you have a financially responsible child, you really should discuss the possibility of this trust with the child before you put it into your Will. Does your child understand how this would work? Does your child want this opportunity to save taxes, or is it too complicated, or does the child have other plans for the inheritance? You may want to have a meeting with your lawyer and your child present to discuss your estate planning.

Example terms of a trust for a financially responsible child:
- The trustee shall generously distribute the income and capital of the trust for the benefit and advancement of the

beneficiary and the beneficiary's children in the trustee's absolute discretion
- The trustee is not required to act with an even hand.

If your child is a young adult, you can provide some capital distributions early in life, then leave the rest in the trust for the long-term:
- The trustee shall have the discretion to distribute income and encroach upon capital for the education, health, benefit and advancement of the child
- Further encroachments as follows:
    - $100,000 at age 25 years
    - $100,000 at age 30 years, and
    - after the age of 30 years, the trustee shall generously distribute the income and capital of the trust for the benefit and advancement of the beneficiary and the beneficiary's children in the trustee's absolute discretion.

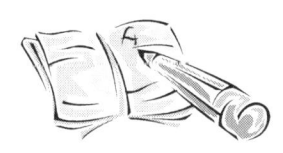

Sample Estate Plan
Retired couple with a large, challenging family

Tom and Jean have been married for 45 years. They have three adult children: Allen, Betty, and Cameron.

Allen is unemployed, alcoholic, divorced and lives nearby. Tom and Jean often give him money. The couple is very fond of Allen's two young adult children, Anna and Andrew. Anna is working at low-wage jobs. Andrew has been in jail, but is trying to learn a trade.

Betty is working, married with two children in high school, and living in another province. She has a prickly relationship with her parents and brothers, and rarely speaks to them. Tom and Jean have not had much contact with Betty's children lately.

Cameron has a successful business, lives in a city 200 km away, and has a common-law wife and three elementary school-aged children (two of them theirs – Clark and Cassidy -- and one from her previous relationship - Zachary). Clark is autistic. The couple visits Cameron often to help with the children. Cameron very much disapproves of Allen's lifestyle.

Tom and Jean own their home jointly. They own their bank and investment accounts jointly. They have named each other as beneficiaries on their registered plans.

They also own vehicles, household goods and personal items. Their combined estate, after projected taxes on their registered plans, is over $1.5 million.

Each Will for Tom and Jean says:
- The first choice for executor is the spouse, and the alternate is Cameron and a trust company
- Upon the death of one spouse, all that spouse's assets are distributed to the surviving spouse
- Upon the death of the last surviving spouse, all the assets (except personal property) are divided into three equal parts. The first part will go into a trust for Allen and his children. The second part will be subdivided into separate trusts for each of Betty's children. The third part will go into a trust for Cameron and his children (including Zachary). All personal property will be distributed at the sole discretion of Cameron and may be divided unequally
- The trustee for Allen and his children is the trust company. The terms of the trust are:
    o the trustee may distribute income and encroach upon capital for the education, health, benefit and advancement of Allen, Anna and Andrew
    o the trustee is not required to operate with an even hand among the beneficiaries

- the trustee shall make payments directly to third parties whenever practical
- the trustee shall not give Allen more than $200 cash at any time and no more than $1000 cash in a month; the trustee shall not give either Anna or Andrew more than $500 cash at any time; these amounts may be adjusted for inflation at the trustee's sole discretion, and
- the trustee shall manage the trust so that it is available to support Allen for his lifetime.

- The trustee for Betty's children is Betty and the trust company. The terms of the trusts are:
  - the trustee may distribute income and encroach upon capital for the education, health, benefit and advancement of the child until the child reaches age 35 years
  - further capital encroachments as follows: 1/3 of the remaining capital at age 25 years, ½ of the remaining capital at age 30 years, and the remaining capital at age 35 years, and
  - if a child dies before age 35 years, then any children of the child become the beneficiaries; if there are no children of the child, then distributed to the grandchild's siblings.

- The trustee for Cameron and his children is Cameron. The terms of the trust are:
  - the trustee may distribute income and encroach upon capital for the education, health, benefit and advancement of Cameron, Clark, Cassidy, and Zachary, and any other children of Cameron, and
  - the trustee is not required to operate with an even hand among the beneficiaries.

This example shows how flexible trusts can be to meet the varying needs of your family members.

What about ME?

If you anticipate receiving an inheritance, then you might want to speak with your parents (or other generous people) about creating a trust for you (and your children) in their Wills.

Your parents may not know about the power of trusts in their Wills. Information like this should be shared!

Chapter Fifteen
Leaving assets to your parents

For many reasons, people often take care of their parents. If you financially support a parent, you can create a trust that continues to financially support the parent for the rest of his or her life.

You can create a trust in your Will that sets aside enough money for the parent's needs. The trustee will pay the expenses to support your parent. Any money left in the trust after your parent dies can be distributed according to your wishes – to your children (or their trusts), your spouse, or to charity, for example.

Of course, there is nothing wrong with gifts to your parents if you are doing your estate planning when your parents are still healthy and vigorous. We hear that parents love to go on cruises, especially when paid for by their children!

Good Planning
Taking care of Mom

Jade is married with children. Jade and her mother, Mrs. Ning, immigrated to Canada many years ago. Mrs. Ning has no other relatives in Canada. Mrs. Ning lives nearby and is financially dependent on her daughter.

In her Will, Jade includes a clause that sets aside $100,000 in a trust for her mother. The trustee is Jade's husband. The terms of the trust are:
- The trustee may distribute income and encroach upon capital to pay for living expenses of the beneficiary, and
- Any remaining capital after the beneficiary's death shall be divided equally between Jade's husband and children.

Chapter Sixteen
What happens to my pet?

Lorraine used to say that her dog loved her the most. Koko was always there for Lorraine unconditionally. Often pets can be like children. They are really part of the family.

If you want your pet to go to a loving home, write down the name of the person who has agreed to take your pet. In your Will, you can say who should have ownership of your pet. Name an alternate person, too, in case your first choice is unavailable.

Taking care of your pet can be expensive, so why not give some money to the person who takes your pet? Maybe $5,000? Maybe more or less depending on the needs, health and age of your pet. Whatever the amount, it is meant to ensure that your pet gets proper care. Naturally, once you give the money to whoever takes care of the pet, there is no assurance the money will necessarily go directly to the pet but that's part of choosing the right person in the first place.

Leaving money in trust for your pet might be going too far . . . although is has been done before – albeit by an eccentric, rich, dog lady.

Chapter Seventeen

Can I leave something for my friends?

Friends can be as important as family. Sometimes friends are closer than family. Family can be far away – sometimes physically, sometimes emotionally. There is an old saying that you choose your friends, not your family.

Why not leave something to your friends to say thanks for the memories or in appreciation of their contribution to the enjoyment of your life?

Through your Will, you can give your friend some cash. You can ask your friend to buy an expensive bottle of wine to toast your memory. In your Will, tell your friend to take that long-discussed dream vacation or maybe give him that classic car he helped you restore. You could give your crafting friends one of your treasured quilts. Who would appreciate it more than someone who enjoys quilting? Your kids may not value your old silverware, but a friend might.

Whatever the case may be, there is nothing wrong with leaving a significant amount of money for a friend. Go ahead, put it in a trust if you want to give the gift of money <u>and</u> income tax savings!

Chapter Eighteen

How do I leave money for charity?

While there are many reasons for making charitable donations, some of the top reasons people give to charity are belief in the organization, commitment to social responsibility, and paying less tax. Giving to a worthwhile cause is good for the soul.

You can give to a charity while you are living, or you can give through your Will. When you have a desire to give to a charity in your Will, there are some important things to know.

Charity versus *charitable foundation*

When you give to a charity, that charity must spend your gift relatively quickly.

A charitable foundation will invest your gift and spend it over a longer period of time. Consider a gift to a charitable foundation if your gift is sizeable. Many charities will also have a charitable foundation. A hospital is typically a charity; e.g., Royal Victoria Hospital, and that hospital may also have a charitable foundation with a similar name - Royal Victoria Hospital Foundation.

There are also community foundations, such as the Edmonton Community Foundation that provide long-term funding to many charities. In Canada, there are over 150 community foundations that provide a flexible and easy way to set up an endowment fund. Municipal community foundations allow individuals and families to create a planned giving program to the foundation in the individual's name or the family's name to provide an ongoing legacy.

If you are thinking of a gift to a charitable foundation, then you should meet with its administrators and sign an agreement that binds them to handle your gift as you wish. For example, you might want to give to a university foundation to fund a scholarship for a specific faculty or program, or to fund research in a certain field. Or you may want to give to a hospital foundation to use your gift to care for patients with particular ailments like Alzheimer's or lung disease. Or maybe you want to give to a community foundation so your contributions are used to fund a number of specified charities.

Creating your own charitable foundation is possible, but requires a very large amount of money (many millions) to be practical. It also requires people who are willing to administer it. A lawyer who specializes in charities can help you create a charitable foundation.

Specifying gifts in your Will

There are many different ways to give money to charities through your estate:

1. Cash amount. Simple and clear
2. Source. For example, the money remaining in a bank account, or the net proceeds from the sale of your car. Also simple and clear
3. Source with limits. For example, the money remaining in your bank account, but not more than $10,000

4. Shares of public companies, mutual funds and segregated funds. Giving these types of investments has the additional benefit of reducing the income tax otherwise payable on your death. When you do this, you will not pay capital gains tax and you will receive a charitable donation receipt for the full value of the investments. This means less income tax for you and more money for the charity or charitable foundation!

5. An amount equal to the funds remaining in your registered funds. When you do this, you effectively give the amount of your RRSP or RRIF, and you get a charitable donation receipt that will offset the amount of income tax you must pay when the RRSP or RRIF is collapsed on your death

6. A percentage of your estate. This is NOT RECOMMENDED. Whenever you give a gift of a percentage of your estate, the recipient is entitled to a full accounting of your estate from your executor. You probably don't want the board of directors, the administrators, and the office staff of the charity to have access to the full financial details of your estate.

Non-profit organizations

You can also give money to non-profit organizations. Not every group or club is a charity, but that doesn't mean you can't give it money in your Will. It just means you won't get a charitable donation receipt. This need not be a barrier to your generosity – after all, you don't get a charitable donation receipt when you give money to your children, either. So go ahead, leave money to your square dancing group, or your old Little League organization. Give your collection of antique cameras to a local museum.

C. Key People in Your Estate Plan

After your death, one or more people need to be entrusted to carry out your wishes. Those people will have different roles depending on the responsibilities you give to them. There are three key roles: the executor, the trustee and the guardian. Each of these important roles is discussed in this section.

Chapter Nineteen

Choosing an executor

An executor is the person who you name in your Will who will have the legal responsibility to settle your estate after your death. Settling an estate takes around 18 months, and maybe more . . . potentially years if you have business assets, adversarial family members, a highly valuable estate, a very low value estate, strange problems arise, or if the executor does not have the time, health, interest or ability to efficiently settle your estate.

The Ideal Executor

The ideal executor can make a big difference in estate settlement. Here are some characteristics of the ideal executor:
- Lives in the same area as you
- Has experience managing money and dealing with financial institutions
- Can deal with your relatives and beneficiaries objectively
- Is comfortable dealing with lawyers and accountants
- Has the time to spend settling your estate which is a part-time job for 1½ to 2 years
- Has the patience to deal with government agencies (especially tax departments)
- Is organized and willing to do lots of paperwork

- Is not afraid to ask for professional help when needed
- Has experience settling estates or is willing to read, research and learn.

In your Will, you should appoint a primary executor and an alternate executor. It is important to appoint an alternate executor because your primary executor may die before you, or may be ill or become ill when it is time to settle your estate.

Married people will often name each other as their executor. Generally, this is a good idea if each Will says that everything goes to the surviving spouse. This might not be a good idea if the spouse is elderly or unhealthy or financially inexperienced. This also might not be a good idea if the spouse is the second spouse and family members from the first marriage are adversarial.

Naming more than one executor

Is naming more than one person as executor (co-executors) a good idea? Sometimes. It could help share the burden if the co-executors work well together. It would not be a good idea if any of them do not live locally – at the very least, it would be hard for them to get together to meet with accountants and lawyers and to sign documents. More than two co-executors is never a good idea because group decision-making is rarely easy.

Using a trust company

Think about naming a trust company as your executor (or a co-executor). Trust companies could have all the ideal characteristics of a good executor. Yes, they cost money, but the money is paid out of your estate. You can enter into an agreement with a trust company regarding their fees. Their fees are usually a percentage of your estate on a sliding scale (the larger the estate, the smaller the percentage fee) and usually start around 5% on the first $1 million in your estate. Trust companies, like any executor, will also demand repayment of expenses incurred on the estate's behalf (for example, legal fees, accounting fees and realtor fees).

Anyone who settles your estate (e.g. spouse, child, sibling or friend) is entitled to be paid, and that payment can be more or less than what a trust company might charge. You can state how much your executor should be paid in your Will, but be aware that your executor can seek the approval of a court to be paid more.

Cautionary Tale
"Good kids" are not always "good executors"

Sabrina is a widowed mother with two adult children. Both children are employed, well-educated, live nearby, and are equal beneficiaries of the estate. While neither of the children is in desperate need of money, they could both use their inheritances to pay debts and maintain their homes and vehicles. In her Will, Sabrina decided to name her children joint executors of her estate.

After Sabrina died, her children were faced with a few assets: the family home and its contents, a car, the RRIF, and two other investment accounts. A year later, nothing had been done. By comparison, a responsible executor would likely have done many significant things in the subsequent year like obtained probate, insured the property as a vacant home, cleaned out the home, distributed the contents, sold the home, changed registration on the car, collapsed and distributed the RRIF, collapsed the investment accounts into an estate account, and filed the terminal tax return.

Why hadn't anything been done by the children? The reasons were numerous. Neither child had any experience settling an estate. Both children were busy and uninterested in settling the estate. Each child wanted the other one to take the lead.

Both children were intimidated about meeting with a lawyer and fearful of the cost of a lawyer.

By their inaction, the children are increasing their risk of loss (by failing to properly insure the home and re-register the car), increasing their tax bill (by failing to pay tax on the RRIF and file the terminal tax return), and incurring the ongoing costs of owing the home (utility bills and property taxes).

These risks and costs will continue until the children decide to act. In the meantime, no one has any power to compel or encourage the children to carry out their legal obligation to settle their mother's estate. Choosing the wrong executors can mean your life savings are simply wasted away.

Executor's Duties

Below you will find a list of things that executors need to do. This list is far from exhaustive but illustrates how important it is to choose a good executor. Remember, settling your estate is not an honour. It is a burden. Choose your executor carefully to ensure that he or she can handle the job.

Immediately After Death
Arrange for organ donation
Arrange for funeral:
    Meet with family
    Meet with funeral director
    Meet with religious leaders.
Review Will with lawyer
Arrange for care of dependents and pets
Find and secure all assets:
    Home
    Contents of home
    Other real estate
    Personal property
    Business
    Vehicle

Perishable goods
Safety deposit box
Obtain insurance for any vacant real estate.

Very Soon After Death
Pay for funeral
Find all ongoing expenses and debts
Stop all unnecessary expenses:
- Subscriptions (magazine, theatre)
- Health care (home care)
- Memberships (gym, club, sports, auto, professional, etc)
- Entertainment (cable, satellite, websites)
- Communication (telephone, cell phone, Internet)
- Insurance (auto, disability).

Forward mail
Notify all holders of assets:
- Bank
- Broker
- Investment advisor
- Insurer.

Notify all service providers:
- Utility companies
- Landlord
- Property maintenance

Cancel credit and debit cards
Review all documents relating to assets:
- Property insurance
- Mortgage
- Lease
- Business
- Investment.

Review all documents relating to financial obligations:
- Contracts
- Divorce or separation agreement
- Court orders.

Soon After Death
Institute plan for securing and managing assets until sale, disposal or distribution
Re-register or transfer ownership of all assets to the estate
Obtain valuation of all assets
Prepare inventory of assets and liabilities
Obtain probate
Schedule payment of all debts.

Within Weeks of Death
Meet with all beneficiaries of estate
Maintain or initiate legal actions on behalf of the estate
Defend legal actions against the estate
Advertise for creditors
Collect life insurance
Arrange for transfer of assets passing outside the estate:
    Registered investments
    Jointly held accounts and land.

Remaining Estate Settlement Process

Maintain records of assets and estate administration
Sell assets, as appropriate
Collect debts
Pay debts
Litigate or settle all claims by or against the estate
File outstanding tax returns (including terminal return)
File estate tax returns
Obtain tax clearance certificate
Obtain interpretation of Will
Distribute assets according to the Will:
    To individuals
    To charities
    To trusts.
Claim executor's fees
Obtain releases from beneficiaries.

Chapter Twenty
Choosing a trustee

A trustee is a person who legally owns the assets you leave in trust. The trustee has special legal obligations, called fiduciary duties, to carry out your wishes for the trust assets as written in your Will or deed of trust.

Since the trusts you set up in your Will could last many decades, you must carefully choose your trustee and set up a mechanism for replacing your trustee if your trustee is unable to continue to act (due to disability from age or illness, or unwillingness).

The Ideal Trustee

The ideal trustee has the following characteristics:
- Lives in the place where you want the trust to be taxed and regulated
- Has experience managing money
- Can communicate constructively with the beneficiaries
- Can distribute money to the beneficiaries according to your wishes
- Shares your values
- Comfortable dealing with lawyers and accountants

- Can commit to years or decades of managing the trust
- Understands tax law
- Understands trust law

Naming more than one trustee

Is naming more than one person as trustee (co-trustees) a good idea? Sometimes. It could help make discretionary decisions easier if another opinion is available. It is definitely not a good idea if any of them do not live locally – it would be hard to get together to meet and to sign documents, and may cause problems determining where the trust should be taxed and regulated.

Using a trust company

Think about naming a trust company as your trustee (or a co-trustee). Trust companies could have many of the ideal characteristics listed above. Yes, trust companies cost money, but you can shop around for trustee fees. Their annual fees are usually a percentage of the trust property on a sliding scale (the greater the value of the trust property, the smaller the percentage fee) and may start around 2% on the first $1 million in trust property.

Executors, trustees, and beneficiaries

Often the executor and the trustee is the same person, but only if it makes sense in your particular situation.

The trustee can be different for each trust you set up in your Will.

The trustee should be different from the beneficiary. If you are inclined to have the trustee and the beneficiary be the same, then get a clear legal opinion of the risks before doing it. If legal ownership and beneficial ownership of the trust property is not clearly separated, then the existence of the trust may be in doubt.

Chapter Twenty-One
Choosing a guardian

A *guardian* is the person you appoint in your Will to take care of your children when you cannot. The Will is the only place you can appoint a guardian. If you do not have a guardian, a public Guardian takes over until someone else applies to a court and gets guardianship.

For many parents, deciding who will physically take care of young children is the most difficult decision.

The Ideal Guardian

The best guardian will have the following characteristics:
- Loves your children
- Healthy enough to take care of your children until they are adults
- Shares your parenting values
- Has a lifestyle that could accommodate your children,

and most importantly,
- Says <u>yes</u> when you ask him or her to be a guardian, if required.

In your Will, try to name one guardian and one alternate guardian, in case your first choice is unavailable or incapable of being the guardian. If your choice of guardian is married, then you probably shouldn't name both spouses (in case the couple divorces – you don't want your kids entangled in your guardians' divorce).

It is not uncommon for new parents to be incapable of deciding on a guardian. If you can't decide on a guardian when it is time to prepare your Will, don't wait until you know! Get the rest of the Will done immediately. Remember that one of the most important times to prepare your Will is the moment you have a child!

Cautionary Tale
The religion barrier

Isabel and Jon had four beautiful children under the age of 9. They both came from large families but only Isabel's brother, Chuck, lived in the same city. Chuck had 2 kids of his own and the two families were very close and spent a lot of time together.

When Isabel and John were doing some estate planning and drafting wills, Isabel thought it would be logical to have Chuck and his wife Ellie become guardians if something happened to them. Chuck and Ellie would be perfect candidates as they were financially capable, they had similar family philosophies about raising children and they wanted to be the guardians for their nieces and nephews. There was one big problem. Isabel and Jon were devoted Mormons whereas Chuck and Ellie left the Mormon church years ago. Jon felt it was very important to choose guardians that would raise their children with the same religious beliefs they had.

This was very difficult for Isabel and Jon and just goes to show how important it is to think through who you want to appoint as a guardian.

D. Dealing with Specific Assets

When you think of estate planning, you naturally think of the important people in your life and how you want them to benefit from your estate.

It is equally important to think about all the assets you own and decide how it would be best to distribute your assets among the people you love.

This next section examines estate-planning strategies, challenges and opportunities with various types of assets that many Canadians own.

Chapter Twenty-Two

Who should I name as beneficiary on my RRSP (or RRIF)?

Whenever you open a RRSP, one of the questions you will be asked is who you want to list as a beneficiary. You should also ensure that the beneficiary designation is accurate when your RRSP is transferred to a RRIF.

It is also important to review your beneficiaries from time to time to ensure that your Will and your beneficiary designations do not conflict with one another. In the case where one designation clearly revokes a previous designation, then the latest designation will govern. However, if it is unclear which designation is intended to govern, then the executor or the potential beneficiaries may have to settle their differences in court, if they cannot do so themselves.

Should you designate your spouse?

In most cases, if you have a spouse, then name your spouse as beneficiary.

There are three key benefits to listing your spouse as the beneficiary:

a. No income tax payable on the RRSP upon your death

b. The RRSP does not become part of your estate thus avoids the probate process and is not subject to probate tax

c. Your RRSP is likely to be transferred to your spouse much sooner than if your spouse is not the beneficiary. Getting money to your beneficiaries tends to happen much faster when you have a beneficiary designation.

Despite these advantages, sometimes designating your spouse as the beneficiary of your RRSP may not make sense. For example, you may not wish to designate your spouse if your spouse has debt problems, or does not manage money responsibly, or is incapable of managing money due to illness or infirmity. In these situations, you might consider instead having your RRSP be directed in your Will to a trust for the benefit of your spouse.

The disadvantage of a trust being the beneficiary of registered plans is that income tax on the full value of your RRSP is payable on your death. However, if your spouse has one of the above problems, then you may have to accept the tax bill to provide for your spouse and protect the after-tax remainder of your registered plan.

Should your estate be the beneficiary?

If you do not have a spouse, or your spouse does not require your registered plans for retirement income, then you could leave the registered plans to be distributed as part of your estate. You can do this by naming your estate as beneficiary or by not naming any beneficiary (in which case your estate becomes the default beneficiary).

There are two benefits of listing the estate as the beneficiary of your RRSP if you do not have a spouse:

- Including the RRSP as part of your estate will add money to the estate, which will provide financial flexibility to your executor. With the RRSP funds, your executor will have a readily available source of cash to pay bills and taxes, and to divide your estate according to your wishes. This is especially important if your estate would otherwise have no cash or liquidity aside from your remaining registered plans.

- Putting the RRSP money into the estate also helps your executor pay for taxes relating to the RRSP. For example, if you designate your children as beneficiary of your RRSP, then your children will receive their share of your RRSP upon your death. However, your estate is still liable for income taxes on your RRSP upon your death, and your executor will now have to find money to pay for those income taxes out of other assets. If there are no other sources of money, then your executor may have a big problem.

On the other hand, the biggest disadvantage of having the estate as the beneficiary of your RRSP is that once the asset forms part of the estate, it also becomes part of the probate process and is available to your creditors. This can be costly in terms of time, money and probate tax.

In most cases, the benefits of having your estate be the beneficiary of your RRSP (when you do not have a spouse) outweigh the disadvantages, but careful consideration should always be made in everyone's unique circumstances.

Should your children, or other people, be the beneficiary of your RRSP?

In general, you should not name non-spouses as beneficiaries of your registered plans.

The limited situations where you might name a beneficiary other than your spouse are:
- You have only one beneficiary for your entire estate
- Your registered plans are small compared to other sources of cash in your estate, or
- You have a disabled, financially-dependent child or grandchild.

Cautionary Tale
Kids as beneficiaries of RRSP

Sometimes naming children as beneficiaries of a RRSP or a RRIF can cause problems. Jack, a widower, named his two adult children, Jenna and Jason, as beneficiaries of a $100,000 RRIF. Jack had only one other asset: a long-held rental house with a basement suite. Jack never lived in the house, but Jason, who rarely worked and had little income, recently moved into the basement suite. When Jack died, his Will appointed Jenna as the executor and gave the house to Jason.

Jenna went to the bank and collapsed the RRIF. The bank deducted a 25% withholding tax, then sent $37,500 to each child. This was done properly.

When doing the father's taxes, Jenna found that the house had appreciated by $200,000. This meant that Jack's estate owed more than $40,000 in capital gains tax as a result of Jack's death. Probate taxes added even more to the tax bill.

The problem is the estate had no money to pay this tax bill because the RRIF asset did not form part of the estate.

Jenna asked Jason to pay the taxes, but he refused with the excuse that he had already spent his share of the RRIF. The tax authorities will demand payment from Jenna, but she is left in a bind. Jenna could either (a) thwart her father's Will and sell the house and leave her brother homeless, or (b) pay the tax bill out of her own money and end-up with less than her inheritance.

This situation could have been avoided completely if Jack had simply left his registered plan to his estate. If he had done this, Jenna would have had $75,000 to pay the taxes, and then she could have divided the remainder among herself and her brother.

By making his children the beneficiaries of his RRIF, Jack left his daughter in a no-win situation.

A disabled, financially-dependent child or grandchild as beneficiary

If you have a financially dependent child or grandchild (due to mental or physical infirmity), then you can transfer a registered plan to this child or grandchild without paying income tax first. Make sure there is a guardian and a trustee in place to care for the child and to manage the registered plan.

A minor child as beneficiary

If you have a financially dependent child or grandchild who is under 18 years of age, then you can direct that your RRSP be used to purchase a special type of annuity for the child upon your death. By doing so, your estate will not have to pay income tax on your RRSP. This annuity must pay annual amounts to the child every year until the year in which the child reaches 18 years of age. The child will have to pay tax on all amounts received.

The tax benefits of this could be significant. For example, a child that is 8-years old upon the death of a parent would pay tax on the annuity payments over the next ten years at presumably lower graduated rates, rather than having the estate pay income tax at higher graduated rates on the whole RRSP upon the death of the parent.

However, there are practical considerations that may be disadvantages. First, the annuity proceeds would have to be managed by the child's guardian without any legal direction or restrictions from the deceased parent. Second, any unspent amounts would have to be given to the child as a lump sum when the child reaches the age of majority. If these considerations raise significant risks – and they often do -- then a parent may choose instead to leave the RRSP to a trust for a child and accept that the estate will first have to pay taxes on the RRSP.

Do not attempt to take advantage of this tax deferral without careful legal advice.

Naming a charity as beneficiary

If you have no spouse, or if your spouse predeceases you, then consider leaving your registered plans to charity. If you do so, your executor will get a charitable donation receipt to offset the tax otherwise payable on the collapse of the registered plan on your death. Your other heirs will get no benefit from your registered plans, but at least the government doesn't get any of it and your favorite charity gets more. Talk to a lawyer about how to do this to ensure that your estate gets the charitable donation receipt.

Chapter Twenty-Three
Joint ownership of bank and investment accounts

When it comes to bank accounts and investment accounts, different couples have different arrangements based on their personal beliefs. Some couples maintain strictly separate accounts while others hold everything under joint ownership.

Joint ownership with your spouse

There are pros and cons to joint ownership of bank accounts and investment accounts with your spouse.

There are some benefits to having your spouse as a joint owner:
- No income tax payable upon your death
- Not part of your estate – no probate process or probate tax
- No delay in your spouse's access to these funds.

On the other hand, the disadvantages of joint ownership are:
- Funds available to your spouse's creditors
- Cash may not be available to pay your taxes and other debts after death thereby forcing your executor to sell other assets
- Funds not available for distribution to other beneficiaries

- Needs careful record-keeping for income tax purposes during your lifetime.

For estate planning purposes, most spouses should have joint accounts unless the disadvantages pose real problems in their particular circumstances.

Joint ownership with a child or other person

There are often reasons why a lone surviving parent might want to have a joint account with an adult child:
- So the child can pay the parent's bills
- So the child can manage the money (e.g. reinvesting expired GICs).
- To leave the remaining money to the child after the parent's death.
- To avoid probate process and probate tax on the account.

Despite these reasons, putting a bank account or investment account into joint ownership with anyone other than your spouse is typically NOT recommended. There are a number of reasons for this:
- Funds are immediately available to this other person's creditors (including in a divorce)
- Funds may not be available to pay your debts after death
- Funds not available to your other beneficiaries
- Careful record-keeping is required for income tax purposes during your lifetime
- Many family fights have occurred over joint accounts.

Generally speaking, the disadvantages of joint ownership with children are greater than the benefits. Be very cautious about putting children as joint owners of your bank and investment accounts.

If you need the regular assistance of your child for bill payment and money management, there is a better way to give your child power over your accounts. Simply go to the bank with your child and give your child signing authority over your account (rather than joint ownership). Another alternative is to set up electronic banking and have your child help you do your regular banking from the comfort of your own home.

If you were considering making an account into a joint account with a child so that the child would receive the funds after your death, then you can achieve the same result with a clause in your Will that gives the account to the child. Even though this may subject the account to probate tax and the probate process, it is cheaper than having your family litigate whether your child is entitled to the account.

Cautionary Tale
Fighting all the way to the Supreme Court of Canada

Surviving family members fighting over joint bank accounts left by a deceased parent has been such a problem that the Supreme Court of Canada had to address the issue three times in 2007.

In these cases, three different Ontario families had the same problem. An elderly parent had a bank account that was made into a joint account with an adult child. After the parent died, another family member challenged the adult child's right to keep everything in the joint account. In two of the cases, the challenging family members were siblings of the adult child, and in one case, the challenge came from the ex-husband of the adult child.

Even though it might be obvious to many people that the purpose of a joint account is to allow the surviving account holder to receive full ownership of the account, the Supreme Court of Canada disagrees. As it stands now, the law in Canada is that an adult child does not automatically gain full rights to a joint account after a parent dies.

Instead, the surviving child must prove that it was the parent's intention to give the adult child full rights to the joint account after the parent's death. Precisely what evidence is sufficient under what particular circumstances was not exhaustively decided by the Supreme Court of Canada.

With this continuing uncertainty, why risk causing a family fight over this issue? Avoid joint accounts with your children and it will never happen.

Chapter Twenty-Four

Tax free savings account (TFSA)

Tax Free Savings Accounts are new for all Canadians beginning in 2009. While most people's TFSA will likely have a modest value for many years, the TFSA may eventually turn into one of the most powerful and valuable savings tool that Canadians ever see.

All the implications of the death of the holder of a TFSA are unknown at the time of the writing of this book because the TFSA is brand new. The various twists and wrinkles of the TFSA will be worked out over time as people encounter novel situations, and the courts, financial institutions and advisers learn how to deal with them. Some general comments, however, can still be made with relative certainty.

Leaving your TFSA to your spouse

Upon your death, your TFSA ceases unless you leave it to your spouse in your Will or via a beneficiary designation (if available). If you leave your TFSA to your spouse, then your spouse obtains the TFSA with all the characteristics (contribution room, tax free returns on contributions) that it had until your death. As your TFSA is valuable, you should always consider leaving it to your spouse.

The disadvantages of leaving your TFSA to your spouse, rather than your estate, are:
- Funds available to your spouse's creditors
- Cash may not be available to pay your taxes and other debts after death thereby forcing your executor to sell other assets (if left to your spouse via a beneficiary designation)
- Funds not available for distribution to other beneficiaries.

Leaving your TFSA to other people

While your TFSA ceases if you leave it to someone other than your spouse, you are free to leave it to anyone else. Specifically, you can divide the contents among as many people as you wish, or leave it to be distributed along with the remainder of your estate. As with any other valuable asset, you should consider whether to leave someone's share to them directly or in a trust.

If available, the benefits of naming beneficiaries directly on the TFSA are:
- The TFSA is not part of your estate so there is no probate process or probate tax on this asset
- Your executor will be able to handle this asset relatively easily.

On the other hand, the benefits of leaving the TFSA to a testamentary trust for a beneficiary are:
- Protection from the beneficiary's creditors
- Control over proceeds after your death
- Opportunity for your beneficiaries to save on future income tax.

Chapter Twenty-Five
Joint ownership of my home

Owning your home with your spouse

Most spouses will own their home jointly.

The benefit of joint ownership of a home by spouses is the avoidance of the probate process and probate tax. As the family home is commonly the most valuable asset in an estate, the savings in time and money are important.

There are some circumstances where spouses will not own their home jointly. For example, joint ownership would not be appropriate if one of the spouses has, or potentially has, problems with creditors (e.g. financially irresponsible or in a risky profession). Another example where joint ownership may not be appropriate is in second marriage situations involving children from the previous relationships who live in the home.

Joint ownership with a child or other person

In general, no one should be an owner of a home who does not live in the home full-time and who is not responsible for a share of the expenses of the home. Consequently, a child usually should NOT be a joint owner with a parent on the parent's home.

There are two coming reasons why a lone surviving parent might want to put an adult child as joint owner of the parent's home:
1. To avoid the probate process and probate tax, and
2. To avoid the estate settlement process, and automatically transfer the asset to the child upon the death of the parent.

However, one has to be very careful about putting an adult child, or someone other than a spouse, as a joint owner because there are some serious potential disadvantages.

- o In most cases, the child will not be eligible to claim the house as their principal residence. As a result, there may be potential income tax consequences. From the time the child is listed as a joint owner, he or she becomes legally liable to pay capital gains tax when the home is sold. A principal residence is one of the few assets that gets preferential income tax treatment, so losing this potential benefit is something you want to avoid.

- o Once a person becomes a joint owner, the equity in the home becomes available to the child's creditors. This can be a particularly problematic issue if the child goes through a divorce. The child's spouse could demand to be paid some of the equity in the property during the divorce.

- o Property is an asset and banks have no problems using property as collateral for loans. When you put your child as a joint owner on your residence, your child can now use the property as collateral for a new loan. If you want to sell the property, proceeds from the sale of the home could end up going towards repaying the loan first.

- o As a joint owner, the child can prevent you from selling the property. You cannot fully dispose of a property unless all the owners agree to the sale and sign the deed of sale.

- o Proceeds from the sale of your home are not available to other beneficiaries. Remember, when you list someone as a joint owner, then the property does not go through your estate. As a result, your other beneficiaries will not inherit any interest in the property.

Due to all these concerns, there are far too many risks in having someone other than a spouse as a joint owner on your home.

Cautionary Tale
Putting an adult child as joint owner on your home

Teresa was a 72-year-old widow with 3 adult children. Two of her kids, Bill and Matt, lived in other cities. Her daughter Sandy lived nearby and was actively helping to care for Teresa.

One of Teresa's best friends passed away. Teresa heard that, before her friend passed away, her friend listed a son as a joint owner of her home so that the son could inherit the house immediately and without probate tax. Teresa thought this was a great idea so she put Sandy as a joint owner of her home.

Sandy was married with two children and did not live with her mother. Sandy owned a very successful business and struggled to try to balance all of her priorities – children, career, marriage, etc. Sandy's marriage started to have problems a few years later. Sandy and her husband finally came to a point where they decided to separate and get divorced. The relationship became so tense that her husband decided to include Teresa's home as part of Sandy's assets, and demand a share.

Soon after, Teresa started to get ill. Bill and Matt started to blame Sandy for their mother's illness — blaming the illness on the stress of her home being attacked by Sandy's ex-husband. Teresa got so ill that she had to be moved into a nursing home. In order to pay for a nursing home with the comforts Teresa wanted, Sandy needed to sell Teresa's home.

When Sandy's ex-husband heard of the plan to sell the house, his lawyer put a caveat on the house to protect his claim. Now, if the house is sold, half of the proceeds from the sale of the house cannot be released to Teresa!

As a result, Teresa and her children decided not to sell the house until Sandy's divorce was settled. However, this forced Bill and Matt to start paying for their mother's nursing home bills and this created more tension between the siblings.

Problems got even worse when Teresa died. Teresa's Will said that all her assets would get divided and shared equally by her three children. Other than the house, which was worth $400,000, Teresa had less than $100,000 in financial assets when she died.

When Teresa died, Sandy automatically became the sole owner of the house because she was the joint owner of the house. Her ex-husband has an even bigger target to attack now – even if he is ultimately unsuccessful.

From the point of view of Bill and Matt, they each have $30,000, after taxes, from their mother's estate whereas their sister now has a $400,000 house and $30,000. Bill and Matt are very upset because they do not see this as being an equal division of assets as stated in their mother's Will.

Teresa's decision to make Sandy a joint owner of her house was not part of a well-considered estate plan. No one should make a similar error.

Chapter Twenty-Six
Dealing with your personal residence in your Will

Assuming joint ownership with your children is inappropriate, what would you like done with the family home? Some people have a great emotional attachment to a house where a family was raised. For other people, a family home is just another asset that can be sold for cash. Your wishes will also depend on the age and needs of your loved ones.

Also relevant to your decision about the family home are the desires of your beneficiaries. Some children might prefer to inherit the family home. Other children might prefer to have the home sold and receive a share of the cash. Balancing conflicting emotional desires of your children can be difficult. Anytime there is a possibility for disagreement among your beneficiaries, there is a real risk of conflict and irreparable damage to relationships. One of the most important estate planning strategies is communication. When deciding what to do with the family home, communication with your children is doubly important.

What are my options?

When deciding what to do with the family home after the owners have died, you have three options:

- Your executor can sell your home and distribute the proceeds according to your Will
- You can give your home to one or more beneficiaries, or
- You can put the home into one or more trusts.

Putting the home into one or more trusts is useful when you want someone (your spouse, your children) to be able to live in your home after your death, but you do not want to give the home to them immediately.

Good Planning
Putting the house into a trust for your spouse

Armondo is retired, owns a home, and has children from a previous marriage. Three years ago, his second wife Geana, had a stroke. Since then, Geana uncharacteristically became irresponsible with money and accumulated some significant debts. Furthermore, because of the stroke, Geana had difficulties with her right arm and struggled to do housework.

From an estate planning perspective, Armondo wanted his children to get the value of the house when he and Geana died. He also wanted Geana to be able to continue living in the house if he died. His concern was that Geana might not care for the home and may even lose the home if he was not around.

For Armondo, the solution was to create a spousal trust and put the house in it along with a large sum of cash. The trustee of the spousal trust is given the power to maintain the home and pay all its operating expenses (funded by the cash). After the death of Geanna, the trustee is instructed to sell the home and distribute the proceeds to his children.

Good Planning
Putting the house into a trust for your children

Adam and Suzanne have two teenage children and one adult child still living at home. Adam and Suzanne have decided that, if they die, the family home should be maintained for the children. Their Wills state that the home will be equally owned by trusts for each child until the youngest child reaches 25 years of age. Until that time, all home-related expenses are paid equally from the trusts of any children living in the home. On the youngest child's 25th birthday, the trustee can decide whether to sell the house, transfer it to one or more children, keep it, or do whatever else is appropriate at the time.

Chapter Twenty-Seven

What should I do with the cottage?

Family cottages often provide memories -- sweet memories of languid days in the sunshine...

A married couple will usually own their cottage jointly. Their Wills should include a clause that decides who gets the cottage after the last of them dies.

Keeping the family cottage in the family is the topic of many books and articles. No one has yet devised the perfect way to make sure that everyone in the family gets *a fair share* of the cottage. Professional advisors, at various times, suggest shared ownership, corporate ownership, and trust ownership. Each has its merits and each is suitable in the right circumstances. You can do these things during your lifetime or in your Will.

Here are three of the most important things to do if you have a cottage:

a. **Start communicating**. Talk to every member of your family and find out what their interest in the cottage is: adult children often have thought about it more than you might imagine.

b. **Create a plan for shared ownership**. If you decide to have more than one family member share the cottage, then set up a plan that stipulates everything about the use and maintenance of the cottage. This is not as hard as it might sound – commercial real estate agreements have been adapted for use by families. An experienced Will, estate and trust lawyer can find one that suits your needs.

c. **Get professional advice**. Get the advice of an experienced Will, estate and trust lawyer to devise a plan to meet your goals and the needs of your family.

Income taxes and the cottage

Assuming you do not live in your cottage full-time, then you will likely have to pay capital gains tax on any transfer of the cottage. This can be a large amount of tax: up to 25% of the increase in value since you purchased the cottage.

If you decide to leave the cottage to someone other than your spouse in your Will, then you should consider where the money will come from to pay the capital gains tax. If your estate will have a lot of cash (e.g. from a savings account, from financial investment accounts, or from remaining registered plans), then your executor and your heirs will not have a problem. However, if your estate will not have enough cash to pay the capital gains tax upon your death, then consider purchasing a life insurance policy that will provide the necessary money.

Cautionary Tale
Taxes on the cottage

When Nancy died, she was a widow and the mother of two children. She owned her own home as well as the family cottage. Both properties were in Alberta where property values had recently increased rapidly. The cottage located at Sylvan Lake was worth about $1.2 million at the time of her death. The cottage had been purchased over 15 years ago for $100,000. When Nancy died, the cottage was left to the two children through her Will. The cottage alone triggered a tax bill of $200,000. There was not enough cash in the estate to cover the tax liability on the cottage so the kids had to get a mortgage on the cottage until they could sell Nancy's home to raise the money to pay the taxes on the cottage. This example shows the importance of understanding the capital gains liability on cottages.

If you own a home and a cottage, it may be possible to claim the principal residence deduction for part or all of the capital gain on the cottage. The principal residence deduction allows you to reduce the income tax you must pay when you sell your principal residence. If you want to claim the principal residence deduction on your cottage, you should seek the advice of a tax accountant or tax lawyer because the rules are very complicated and technical.

If you transfer the cottage to one or more child, then at the time you do so (whether during your lifetime or upon your death) you will be liable to pay capital gains tax at the time of transfer. If the cottage is likely to increase in value significantly from now on, then consider transferring the cottage now and paying your share of the capital gains taxes now. If you do so, however, you risk the cottage to creditors of your children (including on divorce).

An agreement to share the cottage

If you transfer the cottage to more than one child, then you should consider how they would share usage and ownership obligations. And if you do this during your lifetime, what are _your_ rights and obligations? You should seriously consider creating a legally binding agreement (that is, a contract) to answer all these questions before you transfer ownership of the cottage.

If you think your family will have no problem sharing the cottage and don't need an agreement, then consider this brief list of questions:
- Who is putting out the dock in spring and taking it down in autumn?
- Who is painting the deck? What colour?
- Who can be there on the Canada Day long weekend? Can they bring friends?
- Who has to put gas in the boat? Or the barbeque?
- Who has to haul the firewood? Who has to chop it?
- What happens when the canoe is stolen? Or sinks?
- Who should stock the fridge? Who should clean it?
- Who should be hired for winter security?
- What if someone's family wants to spend the entire summer there?
- Can someone park an old RV beside the cottage?
- If someone wants to build a garage, who pays for it?
- How are property taxes and other expenses divided?
- What happens with expenses if one owner lives abroad and uses the cabin one weekend a year, and another owner lives locally and uses the cabin often and whenever he wants?

Can you imagine any of your children having different answers to these questions? Could their spouses or children have different answers?

It is very important to get agreements in place, especially when it comes to families, so as to address these issues and any other issues you can anticipate.

Cautionary Tale
The parents that did no planning

Mom died many years before Dad. They jointly owned a lake cottage where they and their three sons spent many happy summers. Dad's Will was very simple and said that everything he had should be divided equally between his three sons. Dad liked to keep things simple and believed that his sons would figure things out. At the time of Dad's death, the sons were all adults.

The first problem the sons faced was the capital gains tax on the cottage. Dad's estate had very little cash (he was a retired farmer and had given his farm to his sons years ago). The capital gains tax on the cottage was $50,000. Each of the sons had to come up with $17,000 to be able to keep the cottage, which they did.

The oldest son was always the most involved with the cottage: every year he helped his parents maintain and upgrade the cottage, he kept a fishing boat and two snowmobiles there, and he and his wife and children spent more than 20 weekends per year at the cottage. The middle son visited the cottage 6 weekends each summer, but never provided any labour or money for its maintenance. The youngest son lived in another province and only visited the cottage once every two years, but nevertheless he had a strong sentimental attachment to the cottage.

Soon after Dad's death, the sons had arguments over the cottage. The oldest son felt it was only natural that he made the rules since he had the most invested in the cottage. He asked each of his brothers to pay him $3,000 per year to cover the expenses of the cottage. He also asked his brothers to commit to a schedule of visits so they would not interfere with his use of the cottage.

The middle son balked at the cost and noted that the property taxes were only $2000 per year. He wanted his older brother to account for all expenses and he promised to do his share of the work to maintain the cottage. He also refused to pre-schedule his visits since he was an equal owner. The older brother rejected this proposal because he doubted that his middle brother would be true to his word.

The youngest son thought the expenses should be divided based on usage, and since he used the cottage the least then he should pay the least. Neither of his brothers agreed with this proposal!

Within a couple of years, the brothers were barely on civil terms with each other, and there is no prospect that their relationship will improve any time soon.

What about my time-share?

A *time-share* is generally a contractual right to use a vacation property. Many time-shares are sold with the promise that you can pass it on to your heirs through your Will. If your time-share has this option, then you can include a clause in your Will to give it to someone. If you do not specifically leave it to someone, then your executor will decide what to do with it based on the general provisions in your Will.

Chapter Twenty-Eight
Other real estate holdings

A direct investment in real estate comes in many forms. For example, it can be full ownership of a house, or part ownership of some land, or a business arrangement that includes an interest in commercial real estate.

An indirect investment in real estate would be ownership of shares in a corporation, for example, that owns real estate. Estate planning for such an investment is done according to principles that apply to corporations.

Regardless of what your direct investment in real estate looks like, for estate planning purposes you own your direct investment in real estate in one of two basic ways:
- on your own, or
- jointly with another person.

Sole ownership

If you own the real estate on your own, then you can decide in your Will what should happen to the investment upon your death.
- If you want someone to actually have your investment real estate, then remember that any capital gains tax will have to be paid on your death.
- Make sure there is enough money to pay for capital gains taxes on your death if you want the property to be given to your heirs, or if market conditions are poor at the time of your death. Think about life insurance whenever you own non-liquid investments, like real estate.
- If you do not want someone in particular to have your investment, then, in your Will, make sure your executor has the power to sell and manage real estate. By doing this, beneficiaries will not get title to a property that they may not want or be ill-equipped to manage.

Joint ownership

If you own the real estate jointly with another person, then your Will should still address what happens to the investment upon your death (in case you outlive your joint owner), as above. If you predecease your joint owner then the joint owner automatically receives your interest upon your death. You should not own real estate jointly with anyone other than your spouse.

The *inter vivos* trust

If you own real estate on your own, or jointly with your spouse, and
- you anticipate that the value of the real estate will increase significantly,
- you expect to hold the investment for a long time, and
- you want your adult children to benefit from the increase in value,

then you should consider transferring the investment into an *inter vivos* trust for the benefit of your children. This type of plan will cost money because it cannot be done without expert tax and legal advice. Even so, it is not uncommon for people with increasingly valuable investments in real estate.

There are a few key benefits of using an *inter vivos* trust:
1. Shift future value to your children
2. Protect the investment from their creditors (and yours)
3. Avoid estate settlement and probate processes on this asset.

However, also be aware of some of the disadvantages of using an *inter vivos* trust:
1. You must pay capital gains tax at the time of the transfer to the *inter vivos* trust
2. Administrative expenses of operating the *inter vivos* trust
3. Income earned by the *inter vivos* trust is taxed at the highest marginal tax rate (which may not be significant if little income is generated).

Cautionary Tale
The well-intentioned father

Larry made a very expensive mistake. He is a father who bought a small apartment building. He decided to add his 18-year-old daughter on title as an owner. His intentions were good as he thought this would give her some rental income and build her wealth and her credit rating. Everything worked according to plan for 12 years. The rental income was steady and the value of the building rose significantly. In the meantime, the daughter got married . . . and then divorced. Her ex-husband demanded half of the increase in the value of the daughter's share of the building.

The father ended up giving his daughter many hundreds of thousands of dollars to settle the ex-son-in-law's claims under matrimonial property laws.

The lesson is obvious. Don't put your children's names on title to your real estate investments!

Larry could have achieved some of his goals by putting his daughter's share of the building into an *inter vivos* trust for her instead of directly on title.

Chapter Twenty-Nine

In-trust accounts for children and grandchildren

When it comes to putting away money for your kids or grandkids, the financial industry is very quick to offer *in-trust* accounts as a viable option. The other options are either life insurance or Registered Education Savings Plans (RESPs).

An in-trust account is an informal trust so that an adult can invest funds on behalf of a minor. The account is set up in-trust because the child is under the age of majority and cannot enter into a legal binding contract. The adult is then responsible for investing for the child and signing the contract on behalf of the child.

Parents and other relatives often use in-trust accounts to save money for the child. One of the main benefits of in-trust accounts is the money can be used in the future for any purpose and not just for education -- unlike an RESP which can only be used for education. Often the in-trust account is opened so the child can invest holiday or birthday money or the Child Tax Benefits.

In-trust accounts continue to grow in popularity mostly because they are easy to set up, have no legal costs to set up, and have no ongoing legal costs.

A time for caution

As much as in-trust accounts are easy and cheap to set up, remember the old saying that sometimes you get what you pay for.

In-trust accounts are often thought of as informal trust accounts. They are better described as incomplete, ineffective, and ill-advised. The problem is there is simply no such thing as an informal trust. Something is either a trust or it's not. With a formal trust, there are very clear instructions on how the money is to be managed, when the beneficiary can access the funds, and how the assets are to be distributed. This clarity is very important to the usefulness of a trust. In-trust accounts have none of this clarity.

Before you set up an in-trust account, you need to be aware of some very real potential problems.

- o There is risk in using in-trust accounts because they may not be recognized in law without proper supporting documentation. As a result, it is imperative that the paperwork is completed properly

- o Once you put money into an in-trust account, the money belongs to the beneficiary (child). This gift is permanent – there are no exceptions. The whole idea of a trust account is that the money belongs to someone who has rights to the money but is not given the authority to manage it. We've seen many instances where this fact is not understood. Some donors think they can take back the money whenever they need it. Legally, they cannot do so.

- o In-trust accounts do a poor job of defining key things like how the money is to be managed, how long the trust is to continue, and how assets can be distributed to the beneficiary. There is lots of room for misinterpretation and even mismanagement, which will cause nothing but problems and potential conflict.

- When it comes to interest and dividend income, the tax on the income is attributed back to the donor. In other words, the donor has to report any interest or dividend income on their tax return. The only income that is not attributed back to the donor is capital gains.

- You can invest the Child Tax Benefit into in-trust accounts and have the child pay all the tax regardless of whether it is interest, dividend or capital gains income but only if the funds are solely from the Child Tax Benefit. You are better off setting up a separate account rather than co-mingle the funds with other sources. To take advantage of this relatively minor opportunity, you will need excellent record-keeping, or you could face reassessment by the tax authorities.

- The beneficiary (your child or grandchild) takes control of the funds at the age of majority, which is either 18 or 19 depending on the province you reside in. In other words, they can do whatever they want with the money. If they want to use the money in ways you don't approve of, tough luck! The child can take legal action if you decline to give them access to the funds at the age of majority. With a formal trust, the donor defines the age of transfer and control.

- If the donor or the trustee dies before the child reaches the age of majority and there is no stipulation to engage a replacement trustee, the account could remain in the name of the estate until the beneficiary reaches the age of majority. We rarely see powers for replacement trustees put in place, which is very risky.

- If the child dies before he or she reaches the age of majority, the funds in the trust belong to the child's estate. Because minors are not legally entitled to draft a Will, most minors will die without a Will and the child's estate will be distributed according to provincial laws of intestacy. The donor cannot decide who gets the funds in an in-trust account if the beneficiary dies.

o   Since there are no guidelines on how the funds inside an in-trust account should be managed, there is a significant responsibility on the shoulders of the trustee to manage the assets prudently. The problem is different people will have different definitions of *prudent*. If the child feels the funds were not managed properly, the child could take legal action against the trustee.

As you can see, there are a lot of potential problems with in-trust accounts. They are only good for causing confusion and legal disputes. There is never a good reason to have an account that is in-trust for another person.

Cautionary Tale
Setting up *in-trust* accounts for the grandkids

John was very proud of his four grandchildren: Sam, Jay, Phil and Jennifer. John wanted to set some money aside for his grandkids' future and set aside some money as a legacy of sorts. His daughter Sara had already started a RESP for each of the kids so John's financial advisor suggested opening up four separate in-trust accounts for each of the grandkids. This seemed like a great idea because the funds did not have to be used for education only. The advisor said the money could be used for pretty much anything. John certainly hoped the money would be used productively, such as for buying a home, or starting a business, or - best of all - invested for the future. Was opening up the in-trust accounts really a good idea?

When Sam reached the age of 18, he had already dropped out of school and developed a drug problem. John was still obligated to give him the in-trust money on Sam's 18th birthday, which was eventually used to buy more drugs.

When Jay turned 18, he used his in-trust money to take a year off and travel around the world . . . and pay for his girlfriend to go with him. They broke up three months later.

Phil took his in-trust money and invested it into a nightclub business venture that one of his friends started. The venture went sour and Phil lost everything.

Jennifer went to university. She paid for tuition using the RESP that her parents set up. In fact, she got all the RESPs because none of her brothers went to university and the RESPs were transferred to her. As a result, she used the in-trust money from her grandfather to buy a car and some furniture.

John was disappointed with how his legacy for his grandkids was used, except for Jennifer's share. He consoled himself by thinking that one out of four is better than none out of four.

In retrospect, John would have been better off setting aside money for his grandkids in an account in his own name. That way he could have retained complete control of that money. Although he would have lost some tax benefits of having the capital gains taxed in the hands of the grandkids, the loss of tax savings was a small price to pay for having more control and say over the use of the funds. He would have had the ability to give the grandkids the money from that account whenever he wanted to – rather than on their 18th birthdays.

If John wanted the grandkids to get the money when he died, then he could have said so in his Will. The in-trust accounts did John and his grandchildren no favors.

Chapter Thirty
What happens to the RESP?

A Registered Education Savings Plan (RESP) is a special type of savings account created by the Canadian Income Tax Act.

If you have an RESP, it requires special attention in your Will if you wish it to continue for your child after your death. Make sure your lawyer puts in a clause permitting your executor and trustee to continue to contribute to the plan after your death.

Understanding terminology

Before we go too far, we need to establish an understanding of some of the important terms with regards to the RESP.

o A <u>subscriber</u> is the person who creates the plan and who makes contributions to the plan. This could be anyone. However, if the RESP is a family plan, the beneficiaries must be related by blood or adoption to the subscriber. For this purpose, blood relationships include children, brothers, sisters, grandchildren and great-grandchildren. The subscriber is responsible for tracking the total amount contributed to all RESPs on behalf of the beneficiary. Technically, the RESP is the property of the subscriber so if the subscriber dies, the RESP forms part of the estate.

- A <u>beneficiary</u> is the person who will draw upon the RESP to finance their education.

- An <u>individual plan</u> is an RESP set up by a subscriber for one beneficiary. A subscriber may designate anyone as the beneficiary of the plan, including themselves, a spouse or common-law partner.

- A <u>family plan</u> is an RESP set up by a subscriber on behalf of one or more beneficiaries. However, each beneficiary must be under 21-years of age at the time of designation and must be related to the subscriber by blood or adoption. Children, grandchildren, brothers and sisters are considered blood relations, while nieces and nephews are not.

The Subscriber dies

One might think that when a subscriber dies, the RESP would simply transfer over to the beneficiary (child). Although this might make intuitive sense, the rules do not work that way.

With RESPs, the beneficiary is only entitled to the money when the subscriber decides. In essence, the money belongs to the subscriber and not the beneficiary. In fact, the subscriber can choose to withdraw his or her contributions at any time if they wish.

When the subscriber dies, there are four ways to ensure continuity with the RESP:

1. Joint Subscriber. For married couples listing both spouses as joint subscribers is a good idea. Generally the big concern with RESPs from an estate perspective is who will continue to make decisions on behalf of the beneficiary. Appointing a joint subscriber makes it pretty clear and seamless.

2. Appoint a successor subscriber in your Will. If you do not have a joint subscriber, you can make provisions through your Will.

3. Some financial institutions allow you to appoint a successor subscriber at the time of application. Believe it or not, few financial institutions make provisions for a successor subscriber on the application.

4. Provide direction for your executor. The executor is entitled to administer the RESP but more often than not, there is no clear direction for future decisions. Should the executor continue to contribute to the RESP? How should the money be invested? When is the beneficiary entitled to the funds? How much should they get? It is imperative that if there is no joint subscriber, clear directions be provided for the executor.

Should grandparents be subscribers?

Be careful because of serious concerns:

The rules of contribution apply to the beneficiaries and not the subscribers. Subscribers can put up to $2500 into a child's RESP to qualify for the Canada Education Savings Grant (CESG). That limit is based on the child's social insurance number so you can't have the parents putting away $2500 for a child and the grandparents putting away another $2500. It is very important when grandparents want to contribute to an RESP for their grandchild that they communicate with the parents to ensure that someone else has not maximized the RESP contributions. Otherwise, any excess may be subject to contribution penalties.

More importantly because of age, grandparents are likely to pass away before the parents of the child. If the grandparents are subscribers, they should make provisions for ownership, either in their Wills or through a joint subscriber.

Lastly, most grandparents ultimately want the funds of the RESP to go to the kids. When they die, if the grandchild has not gone to school, the funds do not belong to the child as the beneficiary of the RESP. Instead it goes to the successor subscriber. Ultimately, the successor subscriber has every right to cash in the RESP and the money may never get to the child.

Chapter Thirty-One
What do I do with my corporation?

Corporate tax planning and corporate succession planning are industries unto themselves. Complexity, opportunities, and pitfalls are inherent. This discussion is only intended to give you some ideas. Professional advice is necessary and highly recommended.

A corporation is a legal entity generally used for business purposes. The people who own the corporation own *shares* issued by the corporation. If you own shares of a corporation, then you need to consider these shares in your estate planning.
In this chapter, we are only discussing a corporation with a few shareholders, not publicly traded corporations.

Many *ordinary* people now have corporations through which they earn their living. Doctors and lawyers have professional corporations. Business owners, contractors, and consultants have business corporations. Investors have holding corporations. Regardless of what anyone calls a corporation, the shares of a corporation are an asset like any other and can be left to whomever you wish.

Giving shares through your Will

Corporations are technically entities themselves. Consequently, corporations can live longer than the shareholders. Shares of a corporation can be given or sold to your spouse or children. There may be good reasons for your beneficiaries to want to continue running your corporation after your death, in which case the corporation would not have to be *wound up* (i.e. terminated) upon your death.

A corporation may operate the family business or hold valuable investments. It is very important to make sure your Will gives your executor all the necessary powers to operate the corporation and manage the shares of the corporation until they can be distributed to your beneficiaries.

As with all assets, if you give your shares to your spouse in your Will, then you will not have to pay capital gains tax on the shares. However, if you give shares to someone else in your Will, then you will have to pay capital gains tax on the shares. As a successful corporation can be very valuable, make sure your estate will have enough money to pay the capital gains tax upon your death. If your estate is not likely to have sufficient cash, then you or your corporation could purchase life insurance.

If your corporation is not valuable to your beneficiaries, then your Will should give your executor the power to wind up the corporation and distribute its assets according to your Will.

If you have business partners who are also shareholders, then you will want to have an agreement in place to determine what happens when one partner dies. In this agreement, you should answer some very key questions:
- Do the remaining partners have an option, or a requirement, to buy the shares from the estate?
- Does the corporation buy the shares of a deceased shareholder?
- How will the shares be valued?

Smart Tips for Estate Planning

- Do the partners or the corporation own life insurance to fund the share purchase of a deceased shareholder?

Corporate-owned life insurance is a very powerful tool when your estate includes shares of a corporation. When you, or you and your family members, are the only shareholders of a corporation, the corporate-owned life insurance can:
- increase the value of your estate,
- provide cash to pay taxes in a tax-efficient manner, and
- lower the capital gains tax on the shares of the corporation on your death.

You should talk to an experienced tax lawyer, tax accountant, and life insurance agent to explore the options available to you if your corporation owns a valuable investment portfolio (e.g. stocks, real estate, or a business).

The *inter vivos* trust

The following idea is sometimes called an "estate freeze" using a "family trust".

If you own shares of a corporation, and
- you anticipate that the value of the shares will increase significantly,
- you expect to hold the shares for a long time,
- you want your adult children to benefit from the increase in value, and
- you want to transfer a business to a child or children,

then you should consider transferring the shares into an *inter vivos* trust for the benefit of your children. With careful tax planning, an estate freeze can occur without any immediate income tax payable. Furthermore, in the right circumstances, you may be able to set yourself up for future capital gains savings if you manage to sell your shares. This type of plan cannot be done without expert tax and legal advice. It is not uncommon for people with increasingly valuable shares of a corporation.

There are some key benefits to using an *inter vivos* trust:
- Shift future value to your children
- Protect the investment from their creditors (and yours)
- Avoid estate settlement and probate processes on this asset
- Future income splitting of income from the business among many family members.

There are also a couple of disadvantages to be aware of:
- Administrative expenses of operating the *inter vivos* trust
- Income earned by the *inter vivos* trust is taxed at the highest marginal tax rate (which may not be significant if little income is generated), if income splitting opportunities are not taken.

Good Planning
Example of an Estate Freeze

Max and Ruby operate a solid business. They equally own the shares of the corporation that runs the business. The shares in the corporation represent the vast majority of their overall wealth. They have two adult children, Donna and Ernest.

Donna works with her parents in the business and plans to be there for the foreseeable future. As Donna takes more responsibility, the business is expected to become even more successful. She is married with two school-aged children.

Ernest is employed elsewhere and has no desire to ever be involved in the business. He is married with four children (teenagers and young adults). Ernest and Donna get along well.

Max and Ruby want to retire in 10 years and give the business to Donna. They also want to give Ernest "his share" of the business. Mom and Dad will do an estate freeze and create a *inter vivos* trust.

Before the estate freeze:
- Mom has 50 voting, common shares of the corporation worth $500,000
- Dad has 50 voting, common shares of the corporation worth $500,000.

After the estate freeze:
- Mom has 50 voting, preferred shares that are frozen in value at $500,000
- Dad has 50 voting, preferred shares that are frozen in value at $500,000
- An *inter vivos* trust has 100 non-voting, common shares of the corporation worth nothing today (but will grow in value as the business grows in value)

- The trustees of the trust are Mom and Dad
- The beneficiaries of the trust are Donna and her children and Ernest and his children
- The terms of the trust allow the trustees to distribute income and encroach upon capital for the benefit and advancement of the beneficiaries in their absolute discretion
- After Mom and Dad retire or die, the trustees of the trust are Donna and Ernest
- After Mom and Dad die, their Wills divide the 100 voting, preferred shares equally to Donna and Ernest.

This plan allows Mom and Dad to retain full control of the corporation during their lifetime, yet pass along the future value of the corporation to their children.

Chapter Thirty-Two
Other business interests or partnerships

If you operate a business with someone other than your spouse (including your children, siblings, and unrelated people), then you must have a succession plan for the business. This plan must address what happens to your share of the business if you die.

Your share of the business might exist in many forms; for example, by shares in a corporation, loans to a corporation, a partnership interest, loans to a partnership, a joint venture interest, loans to a joint venture, or an interest in property.

There are many ways you and your business partners might want your share of the business handled after you die. For example, you might want your share:
- given to your family
- given to your business partners
- purchased by the remaining business partners
- purchased by the business, or
- sold on the open market.

Depending on the form and value of your business interest, the possibilities and tax consequences will vary widely. You and your business partners need to meet with an experienced business lawyer to discuss your possibilities.

Once you have decided how you want your share of the business handled upon your death, you want your experienced business lawyer to create a legally binding agreement for all business partners to sign.

If you and your partners decide that your share of the business should be purchased, then you might want to make sure the potential purchasers (your partners or the business) purchase a life insurance policy on your life. Thus, when you die, the life insurance policy will provide the purchaser with some or all of the funds needed to purchase your share of the business.

Good Planning
Small Manufacturing Business

Two men were once co-workers who decided to strike out on their own to start an industrial parts manufacturing business. They incorporated a company, bought some equipment, and went to work. Twenty years later they had built a successful business.

They decided that if either one of them died, the survivor should immediately buy all the shares of the deceased.

With the help of their accountant, they agreed upon a formula for determining the fair market value of the shares of the company. Based on the formula, the shares of the company are now worth $1.5 million. With the help of their lawyer, they signed a shareholder's agreement requiring the survivor to purchase the shares of the deceased at fair market value. With the help of a life insurance agent, each of them bought a $1 million life insurance policy on the life of the other.

With this plan, both business partners can be confident that their estates will receive the value of their share of the business. Each of them can now do his own estate planning with this knowledge.

Chapter Thirty-Three
Life insurance

Life insurance is one of the few assets that transfers to beneficiaries completely tax free. As a result, life insurance can be a great tool in the estate planning process.

When you think of life insurance, you probably think it is something you need when you are younger -- when you have dependents and more debts. Many experts have argued that you should only buy life insurance when you need it and as a result, they suggest that you should only buy term insurance. However, we believe that the estate planning reasons to purchase life insurance are much more varied.

When considering life insurance as part of your estate plan, it is so important that you consider four key issues.

1. Do you need insurance?

Just like cereal and milk or strawberries and whipped cream, life insurance and estate planning go really well together. As we said, the most obvious reason why people buy life insurance is to protect their dependents. However, there are other equally important reasons why you might want to have life insurance:
- To cover taxes at death on illiquid assets
- To pay off debts

- To cover final expenses like funeral expenses, and lawyer's and executor's fees
- To provide income for your dependents
- To leave a larger estate for your beneficiaries
- To create a pool of cash to allow your executor to make things equal for your beneficiaries when some things can't be divided
- To help corporations and business arrangements remain viable
- To help businesses cope with the loss of key people.

Obviously, this list is not exhaustive but it does represent some of the key uses of life insurance in the estate planning process.

2. The right amount of life insurance

Once you know why you need insurance, you then need to know the right amount of insurance. This is one of the most important steps in planning for life insurance. Determining the right amount is not always easy. We think it's more of an art than a science. You need enough to meet your goals, but you don't necessarily want to buy more than you need. When in doubt, get help from a professional advisor.

3. The right type of life insurance

The next issue to consider is the appropriate type of life insurance to use. Basically, there are two kinds of life insurance: temporary insurance and permanent insurance.

- Another name for *temporary insurance* is *term insurance*. Term insurance is the most cost effective type of insurance. It is designed to protect you for only a temporary period of time. As you get older, term insurance gets more expensive. Once you reach 70 or 80 years of age, you will not be able to get any term insurance coverage.
- The second type of insurance is permanent insurance. Permanent insurance stays in force until you die. As long

as you pay the premiums, your permanent life insurance policy remains an asset in your estate planning. The benefit with permanent insurance is a price that is fixed over your lifetime unlike term insurance where the price increases as you get older. There are three basic types of permanent insurance: Term to 100, Whole Life, and Universal Life.

Which type of insurance is best for you? The answer is found in your reason for buying insurance in the first place. For example, if you want insurance to pay off your mortgage so your family is not burdened with debt, then term insurance is probably all you need. On the other hand, if you want insurance to create a bigger estate for your heirs, then a permanent policy is probably more appropriate.

4. Shop around

Just like anything else in life, not all life insurance products are created equally. That is especially true when it comes to price. Once you have an idea of what type of life insurance you need and how much you need, it is critically important to shop around for the best deal. If you are not sure how to accomplish that, then seek advice from an independent insurance broker who can shop around for you.

Remember that life insurance is a very unselfish financial tool. We call it unselfish because the greatest benefit typically comes after you die. Life insurance money does not benefit you as much as it benefits other people – usually the people you love most.

Life insurance and estate planning

If you own a life insurance policy, you can do three things as part of your estate planning:
- Name one or more persons as beneficiaries
- Name one or more insurance trusts as the beneficiaries, or
- Name your estate as the beneficiary.

There is no income tax payable on life insurance proceeds by you or your beneficiaries when you die.

Direct to beneficiaries

You can name one or more people as beneficiaries if you want them to have the insurance proceeds soon after your death and without any limitations. You might do this with a relatively small policy ($50,000 - $100,000) when you are confident that the beneficiaries will use the money responsibly.

The benefits of naming beneficiaries directly on the life insurance policy are:
- The death benefit is not part of your estate so there is no probate process or probate tax on this asset
- Your executor will be able to handle this asset relatively easily
- The death benefit is protected from your creditors.

On the other hand, there is:
- No protection from beneficiaries' creditors
- No control over proceeds after your death
- No opportunity for your beneficiaries to save on future income tax.

Insurance trust

You can name an insurance trust (or many insurance trusts) as the beneficiary. An insurance trust works like a trust in your Will. You can appoint an executor, choose the beneficiaries, and decide the terms of the trust. You should do this if your beneficiaries are minors, or if you need to protect them or the money.

The benefits of using an insurance trust are:
- The death benefit is not part of your estate so there is no probate process or tax
- Your executor will be able to handle this asset relatively easily
- The death benefit is protected from your creditors
- The death benefit is also protected from your beneficiaries' creditors
- You can make sure your money takes care of your beneficiaries
- Potential future income tax savings for your beneficiaries on future income earned.

The disadvantages are:
- Paying lawyer's fees for drafting declaration of insurance trust (usually less than the cost of drafting a Will)
- Ongoing effort of trustee to administer the trust
- Ongoing trustee's fees, accounting fees and legal fees.

Overall, the benefits of an insurance trust are usually greater than the disadvantages

Estate as beneficiary

You can name your estate as the beneficiary of your life insurance policy, or your estate could become the beneficiary if you do not name a beneficiary or if the beneficiary you named predeceased you. There are some situations where you might want to name your estate as beneficiary:

- Your estate needs the insurance proceeds to pay your expenses, such as your capital gains taxes (on illiquid assets, in particular)
- You want the insurance proceeds to be distributed according to your Will
- You want to give to charity and obtain a charitable donation receipt.

The disadvantages of naming your estate as the beneficiary of your life insurance policy are:
o No protection from your creditors
o Proceeds become subject to probate tax
o Proceeds become subject to executor's fees.

Good Planning
Responsible dad

John is a hard-working, 35-year old, married father of two children. He purchased a $1 million life insurance policy to help take care of his wife and children in case he died. At the time he purchased the policy, he named his wife as the primary beneficiary, and his children as the alternate beneficiaries. Here's how he could set it up much better.

His current beneficiary designation offers no creditor protection or tax benefits for his wife and children. It also risks the involvement of the Public Trustee (if his wife also dies while the children are minors) and could result in the children receiving money when they reach the age of majority and are still too immature to handle a large amount of money.

John's estate planning would be improved by changing the beneficiary to an insurance trust. A good insurance trust deed, drafted by an experienced Will, estate and trust lawyer might include terms like this:

- The beneficiaries of the trust are the wife and children
- The trustee is his wife. The alternate trustee is John's brother
- The trustee may distribute income and encroach upon capital for the benefit and advancement of the beneficiaries in the absolute discretion of the trustee.

With this insurance trust, no creditor of John, his wife or their children will be able to seize money held by the trust. The trust will be able to minimize income tax on the income it earns by paying income taxes itself or by distributing income to the wife or children, as appropriate. The Public Trustee will not have to be involved, and the children will not receive lump sums of money upon reaching the age of majority.

Chapter Thirty-Four
Your heirlooms, precious things, and household goods

It is normal for people to want their personal belongings to be given to the right people after death.

For your most valuable or precious items, the best way to give something is to mention those items and their intended recipients in your Will. There is no limitation on to whom you can leave your items: people often leave items to their family members, friends and various organizations (e.g. museums).

For all but the most valuable items, the other way to give items is to have a clause included in your Will that refers to a list you may make in your lifetime to guide your executor on the distribution of everything else. On this list, you might give away things like your minor jewelry, furniture, artwork, photo albums, clothing, tools, vehicles, electronics, and anything else.

If your list gets lengthy and has many similar items (e.g. sofas, decorative plates), then include photographs with your list or mark the items with stickers. This will make it easier for your executor and your family to identify each item.

Cautionary Tale
The Kitchen Clock

Sadly, one of the biggest causes of friction among surviving family members is the distribution of the kind of personal property that has little financial value but incredible sentimental value. I have seen a family fight over the kitchen wall clock, which was worth no more than five dollars at a flea market. Sentimentally, the clock symbolized the family home to many family members.

Cautionary Tale
The Doctor's Estate

Dr. Wong started to do some estate planning. His advisor told him that it's not just about the money. In fact there are likely items in his home that one day would become very treasured items. For Dr. Wong's children, one of those items is likely to be his old leather doctor's bag. The bag has no value to anyone except the children, but to them it is an incredible symbol of his accomplishments and identity. Look around your house and identify unique and meaningful items and put them on your list.

Cautionary Tale
Precious Documents

In the past, old photographs, birth certificates, marriage certificates and immigration papers could become points of contention. Fortunately, today, with excellent document reproduction techniques, most documents can be duplicated with incredible accuracy. Still, it might be wise to decide who gets the original and who gets a copy.

Have a system to deal with personal assets.

When it comes to financial assets, it is very common that assets are divided equally. When it comes to personal assets, dividing a grandfather clock or a diamond ring two, three, or four ways typically does not work.

The division of personal assets is likely to be the greatest cause for conflict in families. As a result, it is important that your Will provides a set of rules or a system to deal with distributing personal assets that you have not specifically given to someone. In this system, it is also important to describe a dispute resolution process. Something as simple as drawing names from a hat and taking turns choosing items can be helpful.

Cautionary Tale
The estate system

Lisa is the oldest of 6 siblings. When her mother passed away, some of her siblings fought over certain sentimental family possessions, including their mother's wedding ring, the dining room table (where many family gatherings happened), and a treasured spoon collection. There were many things that the kids did not want and they all agreed to have those things sold at an auction.

The way her family dealt with these items of conflict is they all agreed to have the auctioneer price out all the items including the sentimental items that people were fighting over. The siblings were then given the opportunity to buy or bid for the items they wanted. The cash would then go into the pot and get split among everyone else.

While this was a system to deal with conflict, Lisa always felt it was an unfair way of dealing with things because some families were wealthier than others and what typically happened is the wealthier families got what they wanted.

Lisa vowed not to let this happen with her family so in her will she stipulated that her three kids would be given an equal amount of *play money* to buy items in case of a conflict so that all three kids were on a level playing field.

Chapter Thirty-Five

Loans or advances from you to others

Parents sometimes provide money to children to help with education, buying a home, or starting a business. That money can be an outright gift that no one ever expects to be repaid or accounted for. Other times, the money can be a loan to the child or it can be an advance on the future inheritance.

Loans

If an outstanding loan is possible or expected at the time of your death, you can address it in your Will in one of three ways:

- Forgive the debt, which means that it disappears without affecting your estate in any way
- Demand repayment of the loan. You might do this if the amount of the loan is a large part of your estate and the money is needed to provide an inheritance to other beneficiaries

- Require the amount of the debt be deducted from the debtor's share of your estate and then forgiven. You might do this if the amount of the loan is relatively small but you want to *be fair* to other beneficiaries who weren't lent money.

Advances

If you have given money to a beneficiary with the expectation that the amount is an advance of the beneficiary's inheritance, then you would require the amount of the advance be deducted from the beneficiary's share of your estate. If this is your intention, then make sure you keep careful records of any amounts advanced to your beneficiaries.

Good Planning
Always helping out

Rod and Lara have three adult children. Two children are financially independent. One child, Melody, is 34 years old and lives apart from her parents, but always seems to be short of money.

Melody has been many things in her life: a university student (to be a marine biologist), waitress, dance instructor (modern dance is her true love), retail clerk, dance studio owner, and homeowner (she was *settling down*). Melody has now returned to being a dance instructor.

Melody's parents paid $16,000 for her uncompleted education, loaned her $40,000 for the dance studio, loaned her $80,000 to buy a house, and have given her money often to help pay her bills. The house was sold to pay the dance studio's debts. Melody has outstanding balances on her credit cards, bank loans, and car loan. Melody has never repaid any money to her parents.

Now contemplating their estate planning, Rod and Lara would like to divide their estate equally between their children. However, they recognize that Melody has already been given much more financial support than their other two children.

In their Wills, the couple account for their support for Melody by:
- ignoring the money paid for her education, since they paid for the education of their other children, too
- ignoring the cash gifts, since they did not keep track of them
- deducting the amount of any outstanding loans owing by Melody from her share of the estate and then forgiving the loans, and
- treating any future cash gifts to Melody as advances of her share of the estate.

Of course, Melody's share of her parents' estate will be held in trust for her.

Chapter Thirty-Six
What do I do with the farm?

The family farm is an asset that could have risen greatly in value since its purchase. Consequently, capital gains are an issue in estate planning.

Fortunately, there are many special income tax rules that can help a farmer pass the farm down to the younger generations. These rules allow a farmer to give the farm to a spouse or a child without having to pay tax on capital gains. Since this is one of the few opportunities for a parent to transfer capital property to a child without capital gains tax, the income tax rules are very strict. Always consult an experienced tax lawyer or tax accountant if you want to benefit from these complex rules.

In Your Will

If you leave your farm to your spouse, child, grandchild or ward, then the transfer can occur without capital gains tax payable at the time of your death. This deferral of capital gains tax is available whether you own your farm directly, or through a family farm corporation or a family farm partnership.

During Your Lifetime

You can give your farm to your spouse or a child during your lifetime without capital gains tax payable at the time of the transfer. This deferral of capital gains tax is available whether you own your farm directly, or through a family farm corporation or a family farm partnership.

Good Planning
Hope on the farm

Gordon and Shirley are an elderly couple who lived through tragic circumstances and are now worried for their only grandson, Brent.

Gordon and Shirley are lifelong farmers who had only one daughter late in their lives. Their daughter married and had Brent who was born with physical handicaps. A few years ago, the daughter and son-in-law died in tragic circumstances. Brent was 9 years old at the time. With no other relatives, Gordon and Shirley became the guardians of their grandson.

Despite his handicaps and difficulties with schoolmates, Brent, now 13-years old has a positive personality. He helps around the farm as much as he can, and finds peace in the farm's vast isolation. Brent often expressed his wish to stay on the farm for the rest of his life.

With their health failing, the couple is worried that their farm would have to be sold when they died. Their lawyer guided them through the process of signing new Wills that would put the farm in trust for Brent. Gordon and Shirley had a huge weight lifted off their shoulders now that they had the peace of mind of knowing that their grandson and the farm would be protected from people who might want to take advantage of him.

Chapter Thirty-Seven
What do I do with foreign assets?

Foreign assets come in many shapes and sizes. For example, a condo in Hawaii, a bank account in England, the family home in South Africa, the family business in India, or the secret investments in the Bahamas.

A foreign Will

There are no easy answers when it comes to dealing with foreign assets in your estate planning. Every country has its own real estate laws, Wills laws, business laws, family laws, and tax laws. If you have foreign assets, you are strongly encouraged to meet with professional advisors in the host nation to determine your options and create a plan. It is not unusual to have a Will in Canada for Canadian assets, and a Will in a foreign country that deals with assets there.

Bring assets to Canada

If your foreign assets can be moved to Canada, such as money in a bank account, then you are well-advised to do so before your death. This will save your executor many headaches and will save your estate a lot of money. No one can deal with your foreign assets better than you while you are alive.

Voluntary disclosure

In the mid-1900s, it was not rare for wealthy people to move cash outside of Canada for investment to avoid Canadian income taxes. Not long afterwards, the Canadian government introduced a long line of tax laws to try to force those Canadians to disclose those assets and pay income taxes. Some Canadians never complied. If you are one of these people and you do not wish to leave your family with your mess, then you should seek the advice of an experienced tax lawyer who can submit a "voluntary disclosure" of your foreign assets to the tax authorities. If you do a voluntary disclosure before you are under investigation, the tax authorities will not impose penalties and criminal charges (but you will still have to pay back taxes and interest).

E. More Estate Planning Issues

By now, you should have some ideas about how to start the estate planning process. Estate planning is all about family and giving your loved ones your life assets.

There are some other estate planning issues that don't fit into the categories of *people* or *assets* but are still important to the process. Let's review some of these issues in this section.

Chapter Thirty-Eight
Giving it all away while you can

Giving away some of your assets while you are still alive is a viable estate planning strategy. In fact, it may be a great idea . . . just make sure you keep enough for yourself!

In Canada, you can always give cash without any income tax consequences for you or the recipient. However, if you decide to give something that has an accrued capital gain, then you must pay capital gains tax at the time you give it away.

There are lots of potential benefits in giving away your assets while you are living:

- Seeing happy faces. Giving makes everyone feel good. It's all about the law of reciprocity: what you give is what you get. For estate planning, giving while you are alive can give you a great sense of contribution, satisfaction and happiness.

- Seeing how recipients handle the money. Quite frankly, this could be good or bad. Seeing your children or grandchildren do good things with your financial gifts can be very rewarding. Seeing them make bad choices can be disappointing, but at least you will have more information to make future estate planning decisions.

- Helping and teaching your children or grandchildren to become more financially responsible. Using gifts as a teaching tool is a gift of your knowledge and experience. Financial knowledge is typically passed down through our families, so if you have achieved financial success then you can pass along your financial knowledge as part of your legacy to your children.

- Less assets in your estate means a smaller and simpler estate to settle for your executor

- When you give away your assets, you avoid the probate process and probate tax on assets you have given away.

- Giving to charities while you are alive will provide you the opportunity to reduce your current income tax bill.

On the other hand, there are some disadvantages to consider before giving away your assets:

- When it's gone, it's gone. Be careful not to give it all away at once!

- Less opportunity to use testamentary trusts in your Will which means lost opportunities for creditor protection, managing the assets after your death, and future income tax savings for the recipient.

- Gifts to a spouse or minors can potentially have future income tax consequences if the money is invested. If the recipient invests the money, the income on the gift could be attributed back to the person giving the money or asset away. Obtain professional tax advice before giving assets to a spouse or minor if you expect the recipient to invest the assets.

In conclusion, in the right circumstances, giving your assets away can be a great estate planning strategy -- not just financially -- but also emotionally and educationally.

Good Planning
Widower sells his house

Steve, a widower, decided it was time to sell the family home because he no longer needed the space and could no longer maintain the property. He arranged to move into a rented apartment in a seniors' residence.

Steve lived on a healthy pension, so he would never need to spend the $350,000 from the sale of the family home. Once he sold the family home, he gave a few thousand dollars to each grandchild, and divided the remainder among his two adult children. He also cleaned out the home and gave the children and grandchildren whatever they wanted or needed from the home.

Not only has Steve successfully simplified his estate, but his family really appreciated the gifts. He enjoyed seeing their excitement and receiving their thanks. Steve was really proud to see one of the children pay off his mortgage and the other invest in a second revenue property that would eventually be given to one of the grandchildren when she got married. Steve was proud of this legacy.

When Steve dies, his estate will have far fewer personal items to divide and dispose. His estate is $350,000 less in value, which will reduce probate taxes.

Chapter Thirty-Nine

Alter ego trusts and *joint partner* trusts

Sometimes, the potential for family conflict over your estate can be seen far in advance. When this happens, you need a way to control your assets during your lifetime, then ensure an orderly distribution of your estate with a minimum of conflict. Alter ego trusts and joint partner trusts may be the solution to this problem.

Some people are determined to completely avoid the estate settlement process and probate taxes, but they cannot simply give away all their assets which are necessary to pay their bills and support their lifestyle. Similarly, some people want complete privacy of their affairs and therefore want to avoid the probate process, but they cannot afford to give away all their assets. In both situations, *alter ego trusts* and *joint partner trusts* may be the way to achieve their goals.

Alter ego trust / Joint partner trust

If you want to keep your assets, but keep them out of the estate settlement process, then you can consider a relatively new option: the *alter ego trust*, or, for married people, the *joint partner trust*. These are available only for people over 65-years of age.

These special *inter vivos* trusts were created in the Canadian *Income Tax Act* so naturally the tax rules for putting assets into the trust are complicated, and the terms of the trust must be carefully drafted. Careful planning by an experienced Will, estate and trust lawyer is highly recommended.

The purpose of an *alter ego trust* is to allow someone who is at least 65-years old to create a trust for himself (or herself), and then when the person dies the trust will distribute the trust property according to his/her wishes. By using the alter ego trust, there is no probate process or probate tax, and other people cannot challenge the trust in the way they might be able to challenge a Will.

A *joint partner trust* is very similar, but instead of creating a trust for one person, the trust is created for both spouses and the trust property is not distributed until both spouses are deceased.

Benefits of *alter ego trusts* and *joint partner trusts*:
- Avoid probate process and probate tax
- Avoid challenges to your estate
- Total confidentiality: if your entire estate is in the alter ego trust or joint partner trust, then no probate process will occur and no one will ever know what was in your estate.

Disadvantages of *alter ego trusts* and *joint partner trusts*:
- Can be expensive to set up
- Less opportunity for testamentary trusts in your Will which means lost opportunities for creditor protection, managing the assets after your death, and future income tax savings for your beneficiaries.

In most cases, the cost and complexity of an alter ego or joint partner trust tends to deter people from using them, except for those people with very strong reasons to avoid the probate process, probate tax, and potential challenges to their estates.

Good Planning
Couple creates Joint Partner Trust

A retired couple, aged 77 and 73, has total assets of $2 million, including their home and investment accounts. They have five children and fifteen grandchildren. They have always lived modestly without anyone knowing their business. They live in a province with high probate taxes. They want to distribute their estate quickly and equally among their children and grandchildren. They want to avoid the probate process because they have heard it can be expensive. Given their ages and deteriorating health, they want to know that they have done everything they can to ease the distribution of their estate.

The couple goes to an experienced Will, estate and trust lawyer who creates a *joint partner trust* deed and transfers all of their assets to the trust. As long as either of them is alive, the assets in the trust are at the full disposal of the couple. According to the terms of the trust chosen by the couple, after the last of the couple dies, the assets in the trust will be converted to cash and the cash will be divided equally among their children and grandchildren.

With this plan in place, the couple's estate will pay no probate taxes and their estate will incur no expenses relating to the probate process. No probate application will be filed in the courts. Without having to wait 18 to 24 months to settle an estate, the trust can distribute all of the money to the children and grandchildren as soon as the house and investments have been sold.

Good Planning
The man with a secret

Rick is a financially successful 68-year old who was in very poor health. His doctor suggested that he put his affairs in order. Rick has been married to his wife for more than 40 years and they have two adult children and four grandchildren. Without the knowledge of his family, he has also had a relationship with another woman with whom he has two children, aged 16 and 14 years old.

With the sobering news from his doctor, he was beginning to imagine the problems that might arise from his secret family's appearance at his funeral and their claim on his estate. He wanted to take care of his wife, who was completely financially dependent upon him. He understands that his estate would have an obligation to provide for his secret children who are minors.

On the lawyer's advice, two documents were drafted.

First, the lawyer prepared an *alter ego trust* deed that distributed assets to the wife, adult children and grandchildren upon his death. Into this trust, the lawyer transferred a majority of Rick's assets. The lawyer arranged for a trust company to be the trustee of the alter ego trust.

The lawyer also prepared a Will that left all of Rick's remaining assets to a testamentary trust for his two minor children and their mother. The lawyer arranged for a trust company to become the executor of his Will and the trustee of the testamentary trust.

With this plan, Rick has taken steps to meet his legal obligations to his secret family, and to prevent all of his assets from being subject to claims from his secret family. His wife, adult children and grandchildren would relatively quickly receive their share of his estate from the alter ego trust.

After the plan was in place, the lawyer advised the man to tell his wife and adult children about his secret family. He did so, and his last weeks on Earth were not peaceful.

Chapter Forty

Organ donation

Doctors will tell you that organ donation is vital to their life-saving work.

If you want to make sure your organs are donated in the event of an untimely death, you need to do three things:

- Write down your wish to donate organs, and sign it. Usually, the back of your provincial health care card has a convenient form for you to complete for this purpose
- Keep this note in your wallet
- Tell your next-of-kin (including your executor) of your wishes.

Do not put your organ donation wishes solely in your Will. Often a Will is read too late for organs to be donated.

Chapter Forty-One
Making your own funeral arrangements

There are few things more emotionally difficult in life than making funeral arrangements for someone you love.

One of the best gifts you can give to the people you love is to take away the burden of making your funeral arrangements after your death. Prearrange and prepay whatever you can. In addition, write down all your other wishes.

What can you prearrange?
- Funeral home services:
    - Casket / urn
    - Cremation / embalming
    - Transportation
    - Memorial service.
- Cemetery plot or niche
- Grave marker including the inscription.

What wishes can you write down?
- List of people to inform
- Time limits for completion of burial / cremation
- Information for your obituary
- Location of service: funeral home or church, for example
- Funeral service details:
    - Official
    - Readings
    - Music
    - Flowers
    - Hand-out
    - Charity for donations.
- Post-funeral gathering
- Who should be given your ashes and your instructions for them?

Chapter Forty-Two

How to control your assets after you lose your mental capacity

Whether from a terrible accident or by the grace of old age, you may be alive but unable to manage your finances and assets. To make sure someone is in place to manage your assets, you must prepare a legal document that gives someone the power to act in your place.

Such documents are often called *Power of Attorney* or *Enduring Power of Attorney* or something else depending on the jurisdiction where you live. Such documents may give the power to manage your affairs to someone immediately or only upon your incapacity. Never try to prepare such a document on your own. You should always get legal advice.

Let's call the person you will entrust with your assets your *attorney*.

The ideal attorney has the following characteristics:
- Has experience managing money
- Will manage your assets to protect you and your estate
- Is comfortable dealing with lawyers and accountants
- Can commit to years of managing your assets
- Has the time to pay your bills
- Has the time and patience to communicate with the people who take care of you.

Often, the same person you name as your executor is a good choice for your attorney.

If you do not have an *Enduring Power of Attorney* when you lose your mental capacity to manage your own affairs, then the Public Trustee takes over your affairs until someone else is appointed by the courts. No one, not even your spouse or a child, has the legal power to manage your affairs in the absence of an *Enduring Power of Attorney* or a court order.

Good planning
Husband and wife and three adult children

In their *Enduring Powers of Attorney*, Carlos and Margie named each other as their primary attorney, and then named their middle child, Benji as the alternate attorney. They chose only their middle child because he was responsible, lived locally and comfortably. Their oldest child lived on the other side of the country. Their youngest child lived locally, but had a large, young family and struggled to make ends meet.

Margie became seriously ill and Carlos was able to manage her financial affairs without difficulty. He never had to show his wife's *Enduring Power of Attorney* to anyone because all their bank and investment accounts were in both of their names. After a few months, Carlos also became seriously ill.

Benji, now had to take over his parents' financial affairs using the authority they gave him under their *Enduring Powers of Attorney.* The documents had been well drafted so it was clear that the alternate attorney could take over even if the primary attorney was still alive.

Benji paid all the bills out of his parents' bank accounts, and made sure that GICs were reinvested as they matured. Eventually each of the parents died -- first mom and then dad.

Benji's authority under his mother's *Enduring Power of Attorney* continued until his mother died. Upon his mother's death, the mother's Will became the document that authorized an executor to settle her estate. The same situation occurred for his father's financial affairs.

Chapter Forty-Three

Health care decisions

No one wants to become dependent on others, but the reality is it will happen to a lot of us. Who decides when you get put into a nursing home? Who decides what nursing home? You might be the person needing the care or you might be the caregiver. Anyone who has faced these issues on either side of the situation knows how difficult it is to make these decisions.

Moving you into a nursing home is usually a decision that is made by someone else. How will they know how to make that decision without some direction or knowledge about what you want?

In order to provide that direction, you need to have a *Health Care Directive, a living Will*, or *a personal directive* (they are terms used in different regions for the same purpose). With this document, you give someone the power to make health care decisions for you when you are no longer able to do so yourself.

The ideal decision-maker has the following characteristics:
- Knows how you would want to be treated
- Shares your values about health care and quality-of-life
- Will be available to meet with doctors and nursing home/hospital staff

- Is comfortable dealing with doctors and other health care providers
- Can handle the emotional burden of caring for you
- Can communicate with your other family members.

Name a primary decision-maker and an alternate in your *Health Care Directive.*

Often the first choice is your spouse. For an alternate, people often choose among parents (if not too elderly), siblings, or adult children.

A *Health Care Directive* can also specify the types of treatment or care that you do or do not want. My experience speaking with many doctors who have been faced with these documents is that it is wiser to not specify anything. Unless you have a health care treatment history and know what you will likely suffer from, don't specify anything. No one knows what may befall you and when, and no one can predict what health care would be appropriate at that time. The wishes that some people put into heath care directives (e.g. *no heroic efforts to resuscitate*) are notoriously difficult to interpret, and therefore best avoided completely.

Cautionary Tale
Too many cooks spoil the broth

Belinda, a widow, had an adult son and daughter. She was very unsure who to appoint as her health-care decision-maker. Her daughter was a very busy professional who adored her mother, but lived in the United States. Her son lived locally and helped his mother with her daily tasks and needs. The widow loved her children equally, of course, and did not want to treat them differently. She appointed both of them as her joint health-care decision-makers.

Belinda developed Alzheimer's and could no longer live independently, even with the help of home-care professionals and her son. The son thought it would be best to move his mother into a nursing home. He told this decision to his sister and she immediately became very upset. The daughter thought her mother should not be moved into a nursing home, but instead more home-care help should be hired. Without the authority to make a decision on his own, the son struggled for months to help his mother and to find more help. No more home-care help could be found.

Stressed and exhausted, the son again told his sister that a nursing home was the only option. Again, his sister refused to allow it unless she first visited the potential nursing homes. However, she could not take time off work for a few months, at least.

Both children, acting under great emotional strain and both believing they had their mother's best interests at heart, became argumentative and accusatory. After many tense and unpleasant telephone calls with no resolution in sight, the son went to see his lawyer.

The son's lawyer filed court documents seeking sole guardianship of the mother by the son. Upon receipt of these documents, the daughter became distraught and angry. The daughter eventually consented to moving her mother to a nursing home and the court proceedings were stopped. Thereafter, the daughter grudgingly consented to whatever decisions her brother made, but their relationship had deteriorated permanently.

The moral of this story? Just choose one child as your health-care decision-maker, and tell your children the practical reasons why you made your decision. In addition, help your children to make your future health care decisions by discussing your wishes with them. For example, if Belinda had told her children that she was OK going into a home and the last thing she wanted was to be a burden to them, then having this information may have prevent some of their conflict. Belinda probably would have preferred a decision one way or the other just to keep a good relationship between her children. Think about how you want to be cared for and communicate those wishes with your family.

Chapter Forty-Four

What is your legacy?

In estate planning, the word *legacy* is often used because legacy means that you will be remembered long after you die. Often when we think of legacy, we think of examples of the public legacies of renowned Canadians like Sir John A. MacDonald, Alexander Graham Bell, Frederick Banting, Lester B. Pearson, Terry Fox, and Tommy Douglas.

As great as these individuals were, everyone has a legacy to leave. We all have stories to tell. We all live a life with good memories. We all have an audience that wants to hear our words.

The gift of family

Family is a gift. When you think of your ancestors, do you wish you knew more about your parents, uncles, aunts, grandparents, and great grandparents? They all had legacies to leave, but few of them diarized their legacies for posterity. We have all heard of time capsules, photo albums, and scrapbooks, and these are all examples of efforts to create memories and personal legacies.

Unfortunately, it is usually after the death of a loved one that people often realize how much family history has been lost. It is then that families wished they had diarized the stories and memories of the deceased in an organized way.

Since one of the most important things in life is family, knowing your family history adds a significant dimension to your own life. We all wish we knew more about our family history, so consider the fact that you have the opportunity to create your family's legacy for future generations. Take this opportunity and start creating your personal legacy for your descendants.

Good Planning
Lorraine's life legacy for her grandchildren

Lorraine was a dependent adult for 6 years starting at the age of 56. During the last part of her life, her oldest son Jim fell in love and got married and then was expecting his first child. Lorraine was very happy for her son, knowing that he married a wonderful person and now was going to start a family. Lorraine died 5 months before her grandson, Robbie, was born. Jim was saddened by the fact that Robbie never got the opportunity to meet his grandmother.

When Lorraine died, Jim wanted to make sure that Robbie and the rest of his children and their children and their children's children would know something about Lorraine. Most people in this country would have never heard about Lorraine. She was not famous and she had no public legacy. For Lorraine, she did not need to be famous to have a legacy. Lorraine has a personal legacy, one that is meaningful to her family.

When Lorraine passed away, Jim mourned by putting together a book about the story of her life using stories, pictures, and articles. This book was not only a tribute to his mother, but also his gift to her family including the grandchildren and great grandchildren she never got to meet in person.

Lorraine, like most people, never left her personal legacy. Unfortunately, some of her legacy died with her. Jim did his best to create that personal life legacy, but without her help, unfortunately, some of her memories and experiences were lost forever.

You have the opportunity to set the precedence for the future. If you wish that you knew more about your ancestors, then it is pretty likely that your kids and grandkids will eventually also want to know more about your life. Generations to come will treasure your memories and your stories.

Take the time to diarize the stories of your life. You might laugh or cry, chuckle, or shed a tear as you try to remember the stories of your life. Whatever the case, a legacy of memories is far more valuable than any financial gifts. A gift of memories ignites imagination and fosters communication among families. This should be the cornerstone of your estate planning. It is these stories that bring generations together. No amount of money can weave generations together like a legacy of memories.

The solution

Take a piece of paper and start writing the stories of your life. Take a video camera and start recording. Take a tape recorder and start dictating. These words, videos, or recordings could be the best gift you leave because it will be your personal legacy. Future generations are guaranteed to treasure your gift.

In the end, estate planning is really about preserving memories from the past and preserving financial security for the future. Life is not just the passing of time - life is the collection of experiences. It is about communication. Take the time to connect with your families ... before it is too late!

45 Concluding remarks

Is your brain overloaded with information? When it comes to estate planning, there is a lot to think about. The problem is you can't do everything by yourself and all at once. Our hope is that reading this book brought you many *light bulb* moments. These *light bulb* moments are really important because they represent opportunities to affect your life and the life of your loved ones in profound ways.

Everyone needs an estate plan. If you are one of the many Canadians who have not done any estate planning, then hopefully this book will get you thinking and motivate you to act. We hope you recognize the importance of having a Will, an Enduring Power of Attorney and a Health Care Directive as the foundation of your plan.

If you already have a Will, then maybe we helped you confirm that you have done the right things, or maybe we have helped you recognize some areas that need improvement.

Many estate planning books teach people about trusts and how they can be used as part of an estate plan. We worked very hard trying to simplify this complicated topic so that you can better understand the advantages and disadvantages of the different ways trusts can be used to benefit your loved ones.

Estate planning is all about people and family, that's why we do it. It brings families closer together because family members want to support each other, help each other, and provide for each other.

We hope you better understand the best way to give assets to your beneficiaries. The financial side of estate planning is all about minimizing tax, keeping things simple and problem free, and getting the right assets to the right people in the most efficient way possible.

We hope you understand that estate planning is not just about dying but also about how to make sure important decisions (both financial and health decisions) can be made if you are not able to make your own decisions. Estate planning should include health care planning and funeral planning.

We hope you recognize that it is very difficult to carry out estate planning without good professional help. Having experienced advisors on your team will make all the difference.

And finally, we hope you recognize that everyone has a legacy to share and part of estate planning includes planning to leave a personal legacy. A personal legacy ensures that your family and loved ones can know you and remember who you were as a person, what your life stood for, and the wisdom of your experiences.

The Best Idea . . .

Estate planning is about a lot of things and now you know a lot more about it. Hopefully you have lots of ideas to improve your own estate plan. Knowledge is power but it is not everything. In fact, knowledge is not enough, you must also take action. The best idea is the implemented idea. Not only do we hope you gained knowledge, but that we inspired you to take action. Good luck!

Estate Planning Seminars and Workshops

Marvin and Jim are both exciting and dynamic speakers that speak from the heart.

Estate planning seminars don't have to be dry and technical. In fact, Marvin and Jim prefer to give presentations that are fun, interesting and extremely insightful – even on the topic of estate planning.

In their presentations, you will learn about the do's and don'ts of estate planning. There are so many issues that come into play when someone dies. The key is to be prepared with knowledge and a plan. Marvin and Jim's workshops will help you avoid costly mistake, save money on taxes and fees and maintain family harmony. The foundation of their message is that estate planning is all about family. It's about making sure you take care of the people you love and that your wealth and possessions get passed on in the most effective way.

Marvin and Jim have a whole myriad of topics to choose from: Financial planning, estate planning, retirement, investing, wealth and so much more.

To hire Marvin or Jim for your next conference or meeting, email feedback@wealthwebgurus.com

Good Research Leads to Good Decisions

Marvin and Jim are committed to helping people make better decisions about money. Education is the root of success. Not only are they helping people through their books and their workshops, you can find more resources through some websites:

www.WealthWebGurus.com

WeathWebGurus.com is one of the leading resource centers for timeless planning information on building, protecting and managing wealth. The web site contains over a thousand articles written by various experts on financial, retirement, investment, estate, tax and lifestyle planning. The focus of these articles and all of the information you will find on the site is to provide timeless planning information.

www.MyEstateOrganizer.com

MyEstateOrganizer.com is the home of the software program My Estate Organizer (MEO) that is software that helps people organize, diarize and communicate their estate affairs. It's a tool that reduces family conflict, bridges communication between generations and helps executors and beneficiaries during the difficult time of losing someone they love.

MEO is a tool that sets the stage for financial, retirement and estate planning. It's been said that very few people are prepared for retirement because of lack of planning. My Estate Organizer sets the foundation for all forms of financial planning. It will help people working with professionals to create great plans and move towards financial independence.

Smart Tips for Estate Planning

If you have found this book to be helpful, then please don't keep it a secret. We wrote the book with a purpose – to help people not only avoid making mistakes in estate planning but also to motivate people to simple action.

We need to protect families from conflict and ensure that our possession and wealth go to the right places.

For single orders, please visit:

www.wealthwebgurus.com

For discounts on bulk orders, please contact us directly at Booksales@wealthwebgurus.com

Made in the USA
Charleston, SC
24 February 2011